DATE DUE

MAY 1 1 2015			
NOV 1 7 2015			

Anorexia

Other books in the At Issue series:

DISCARD

Anorexia

Karen F. Balkin, *Book Editor*

Bruce Glassman, *Vice President*
Bonnie Szumski, *Publisher*
Helen Cothran, *Managing Editor*

GREENHAVEN PRESS
An imprint of Thomson Gale, a part of The Thomson Corporation

Detroit • New York • San Francisco • San Diego • New Haven, Conn.
Waterville, Maine • London • Munich

LIBRARY OF CONGRESS CATALOGING-IN-PUBLICATION DATA

Anorexia / Karen F. Balkin, book editor.
  p. cm. — (At issue)
Includes bibliographical references and index.
ISBN 0-7377-2178-2 (lib. bdg. : alk. paper) — ISBN 0-7377-2179-0 (pbk. : alk. paper)
  1. Anorexia nervosa. 2. Anorexia nervosa—United States. I. Balkin, Karen F., 1949– . II. Series: At issue (San Diego, Calif.)
RC552.A5A5472 2005
362.2'5—dc22   2004061693

Printed in the United States of America

Contents

Introduction

Online support groups offer help for almost any physical, psychological, or emotional problem. Proanorexia—called "pro-ana"—Web sites have become one of the most controversial of all Internet support groups. Such sites provide bulletin boards and chat rooms where visitors can post messages, seek advice, and share ideas about anorexia. Increasing in direct proportion to the growing number of anorexics, pro-ana sites are seen by some as a desperately needed source of sanctuary and by others as a disturbing, destructive cyberspace phenomenon.

Karen Dias, a Vancouver, British Columbia, therapist who has worked extensively with sufferers of anorexia and who has had personal experience with disordered eating, argues that pro-ana Web sites serve an important purpose: providing women and girls with a safe forum where they can discuss "ana" and share information. She says, "They make it clear that their purpose is to support those who are struggling with an eating disorder, and to provide a 'space' free from judgment, where they can offer encouragement to those who are not yet ready to recover." She argues that far from the "in denial" portrayals of anorexic women common in medical literature, those who post messages on pro-ana sites are articulate and highly aware of their circumstances. They write poignantly of feeling misunderstood, out of control, isolated, and in pain. Pro-ana Web sites offer the safety of cyberspace and an understanding ear that is unavailable elsewhere, she maintains. Dias suggests that the less intimidating atmosphere of an anonymous chat room gives girls and women the support they need until they are ready for the more intense face-to-face interaction of therapy. "With the pro-anorexia sites, you don't feel like people are going to be judging you," says Liz, a high school senior from Oak Park, Illinois, who frequents pro-ana sites.

Most pro-ana sites also provide online diaries, tips and tricks for dieting—many of which appear as well in mainstream beauty and fashion magazine—and "trigger pics"—pictures of ultrathin, emaciated women—the ideal that visitors want to attain. While the features of pro-ana sites may appear to encourage anorexia, Dias maintains that this is not the case. Pro-ana sites are definitely not in the business of recruitment, she insists, and in fact, warn away those who are not anorexic or who are actively trying to recover. Most sites carry an alert on the first page warning viewers to enter at their own risk because they will encounter proanorexia material that could trigger relapse in a recovering anorexic.

However, many therapists, medical professionals, recovered anorexics, and parents of anorexics disagree with Dias's positive view of pro-ana Web sites and are violently opposed to them. Bob Berkowitz, medical director of the Weight and Eating Disorders Program at the University of Pennsylvania in Philadelphia, likens pro-ana sites to support groups that help people stay sick. He comments, "These sites don't make sense in terms of getting well. . . . It's like recovering alcoholics going to a bar together."

Psychotherapist Steven Levenkron, author of *The Best Little Girl in the World* and *Anatomy of Anorexia*, agrees with Berkowitz's evaluation. He argues further that the sites are dangerous because they help disordered girls and women feel normal and connected with the world and thus diminish the likelihood that anorexics will seek treatment. He contends,

> The problem is, there are lots of girls who are very treatable. But when they get on to these sites they are less treatable. The girls who run these sites are lonely, and instead of calling themselves sick, they get to feel like they have a career. . . . Many of them have no social life, and their only hope is to find other anorexics. But it's negative energy coalescing: It seduces girls into anorexia, and makes the girl who runs it feel less lonely.

Even though pro-ana Web site advocates like Dias insist that the sites do not recruit girls and women into anorexia, the seduction potential of the sites cannot be denied, according to many experts. Vivian Meehan, president and founder of the National Association of Anorexia Nervosa and Associated Disorders (ANAD), argues that "one of the primary goals of anorexics is to persuade others that they are perfectly fine and have the right to lead their lives however they see fit. And one of the ways of doing it is to find other people who are achieving those goals—so these Web sites provide reinforcement, along with a forum for picking up and exchanging tips."

Julie Dekergommeau, a recovered anorexic from Canada, insists that pro-ana sites are so dangerous that they should be eliminated from the Internet. She says, "They're wrong and they need to be taken off the Web. They promote pain and suffering, and in a messed-up way they promote death." She is not alone in that assessment. In July of 2001 ANAD requested that Yahoo!, the host of more proanorexia sites than any other Internet provider, take down its pro-ana sites. While the company offers no other explanation, it insists that ANAD's request was not the reason it took down twenty-one pro-ana sites. However, most of the sites reappeared shortly with other hosts or under names that disguised their true content, demonstrating the importance of the sites to anorexics and the tenacity with which people with disordered eating will fight to keep them.

Whether pro-ana Web sites are helpful or harmful to anorexics is just one aspect of the controversy surrounding this dangerous and sometimes deadly disorder that affects between 5 and 10 million Americans.

1

Anorexia: An Overview

Harvard Mental Health Letter

Published by Harvard Medical School, the Harvard Mental Health Letter *provides information, current thinking, and debate on mental health issues for psychiatrists, psychologists, social workers, and therapists of all kinds.*

While doctors and researchers are not in agreement as to the causes of anorexia, the symptoms and effects are universally recognized. Girls and young women who suffer from anorexia—over 90 percent of anorexics are female—typically refuse to maintain a normal weight, show intense fear of gaining weight, and exhibit a distorted idea about their own body size and shape. Depression, anxiety, irritability, and insomnia often accompany anorexia. Low body temperature, heart rate, and blood pressure are also common. Some anorexics die from cardiac arrest or commit suicide. Until recently, eating disorders were considered a modern Western phenomenon, but research has shown that anorexics lived in previous centuries and in different parts of the world.

It usually starts with a diet. A teenage girl or young woman begins to eat less and less. She skips meals or takes only tiny portions, often avoiding all but a few kinds of food. She may weigh and measure her food, chew it at length and spit it out, or secretly pocket it and throw it away. Sometimes she uses laxatives and diuretics, or makes herself vomit after meals, and she often exercises compulsively as well. She may say that she looks or feels "fat" although she is obviously becoming emaciated. Her weight sinks and her health deteriorates, but she persists in denying that anything is wrong. She may try to conceal her problem by wearing baggy clothes and avoiding other people.

This demoralizing, debilitating, and sometimes deadly condition is anorexia nervosa. Although the Greek and Latin roots of the words mean "lack of appetite of nervous origin," that description is not quite accurate. Appetite—which is often normal, at least at first—is not even mentioned in the standard psychiatric definition. Researchers are still trying to learn why these women want to starve themselves and how to prevent them from succeeding.

A person with anorexia is likely to be depressed, anxious, irritable, and insomniac. Her joints may become swollen, her hair and skin dry, her nails brittle. She is often lethargic and constipated. She loses bone mass (sometimes permanently), and if she is young enough, her sexual development may be arrested. Most important, her body temperature, heart rate, and blood pressure can fall to dangerously low levels. Loss of potassium may cause heart arrhythmias. Death from cardiac arrest can occur, as can suicide.

> " A person with anorexia is likely to be depressed, anxious, irritable, and insomniac. "

About one in 200 persons in the United States will develop anorexia nervosa at some time. Ninety percent are women. On average, the diagnosis is first made at age 18, but symptoms may arise in much older and much younger people. People with anorexia have a high rate of bulimia, the bingeing and purging syndrome. They are also susceptible to major depression (a rate of 50%–75%) and obsessive-compulsive disorder (a 25% rate).

Symptoms of Anorexia Nervosa

A person has anorexia nervosa when:

• She (or, occasionally, he) refuses to maintain weight at a normal level. Her weight is 15% below the healthy minimum.

• She shows intense fear of gaining weight or becoming fat.

• She has disturbed ideas about her weight or body shape, tends to judge her value as a person by her weight or body shape, or denies that her weight loss is a serious problem.

• If she is a woman of the appropriate age, she has not

menstruated for at least three consecutive cycles.

Anorexia nervosa takes two forms:

• Restricting (dieting, fasting, and compulsive exercise)

• Binge eating/purging (deliberate vomiting or misuse of laxatives, enemas, or diuretics in addition to dieting, fasting, and exercise).

The Genetic Background

Eating disorders run in families. In one recent study, the risk for anorexia in relatives of a person with the disorder turned out to be 11 times higher than average. Studies comparing identical with fraternal twins indicate that the heritability of anorexia (the proportion of individual variability associated with genetic difference) is about 55%.

These statistics have inspired a search for susceptibility genes. Last year [2002], European researchers announced that 11% of anorexics, compared to 4.5% of controls, carried a certain form of the gene for a hormone that stimulates appetite. According to a 2002 report, some people with the restricting type of anorexia nervosa (those who don't binge and purge) have an unusual variant of a gene that affects the reabsorption of the neurotransmitter norepinephrine.

About one in 200 persons in the United States will develop anorexia nervosa at some time.

A strain of hogs bred for low fat may provide further data on anorexia susceptibility genes. Some of the hogs are highly active, eat little, and waste away. Researchers are trying to learn whether any similar genetic patterns occur in people suffering from anorexia.

Psychology of Self-Starvation

Physicians have been speculating inconclusively about the psychological roots of anorexia for hundreds of years. Especially in the 20th century, they've suggested a wide range of possible influences, from peer pressure to sexual anxieties and child abuse.

According to one theory, anorexia is a kind of addiction.

The German word for the disorder, Pubert tsmagersucht, means "craving for thinness at puberty." One striking characteristic drug addicts and anorexics often have in common is denial—unwillingness to admit that they have a problem. But most experts find more dissimilarities than similarities between anorexia and substance abuse.

There may be something like an anorexic personality, however. Girls and women with the disorder are often shy, neat, quiet, conscientious, and hypersensitive to rejection. They are prey to irrational guilt, feelings of inferiority, and obsessive worrying. They have unrealistic hopes of perfection and feel as though they can never meet their own standards.

> **// Girls and women with the disorder are often shy, neat, quiet, conscientious, and hypersensitive to rejection. //**

Anorexia could be a way some young women with this kind of personality respond to the demands of adulthood. They don't want to be average or admit weakness, but they fear asserting themselves. Their sexual desires and the prospect of independence from their families frighten them. Instead of acknowledging their fears, they try to restore order to their lives by manipulating their weight with compulsive fasting and physical activity.

In that way they exercise some control over their lives. By denying their own physical needs, they show that they won't allow others to dictate them. Falling numbers on the scale are an achievement—a victory over themselves and others. At the same time, by starving themselves and preventing menstruation, they convey the message they don't want to grow up yet.

Some clinicians who treat anorexia believe that, in adolescents at least, the blame lies with parents who make conflicting demands. The theory is that the parents, in effect, tell their daughter to show a capacity for adult independence without separating herself from the family. In the family systems theory of anorexia, it's seen as a defense that maintains the family's otherwise precarious stability. A daughter who refuses to eat may be trying to hold a disintegrating family together by providing a common object of concern for her parents. Or, just the opposite—the family may be "enmeshed," meaning that its boundaries and responsibilities are not distinct. Its members are overprotective of one another; they don't acknowledge feelings or resolve conflicts. According to this theory, anorexia may arise if the family's rules and roles are too inflexible to change as a daughter grows up.

Fasting and Culture

It's sometimes said that eating disorders in general and anorexia nervosa in particular are largely products of modern Western upper-class and middle-class society. "You can't be too rich or too thin," as the Duchess of Windsor is supposed to have said. In industrial countries, the average woman is becoming heavier, while the body regarded as ideal for health and beauty becomes slimmer. Being happy and successful, women are told, goes with being thin. As a result, more than half of American women, including many young girls, say they are on a diet.

Of course, the vast majority of people who diet don't have an eating disorder. But the more intense this kind of social pressure is, the more likely it seems that a troubled young woman will develop anorexia rather than (or in addition to) other psychiatric symptoms. And now, the argument goes, anorexia, along with bulimia and obesity, is beginning to infect the non-Western world, carried by television, films, and advertisements.

> *Symptoms that would now be called anorexia nervosa were reported as early as the 17th century in England.*

But research has shown that it's not so simple. Symptoms that would now be called anorexia nervosa were reported as early as the 17th century in England. Descriptions of similar symptoms also appear in ancient Chinese and Persian manuscripts and in African tribal lore. Today, many studies show no clear relationship between severe eating disorders and social class or the influence of Western culture.

There is some (disputed) evidence that women in non-Western countries are, on the average, less dissatisfied with their bodies, but that doesn't necessarily imply a lower probability of anorexia. In the United States, whites report more mild eating disturbances than African Americans, but the two groups have about the same rate of clinical eating disorders, including anorexia. Although middle-class anorexia patients may get more attention, it has not been shown that anorexia is a function of social class, either.

> **❝** *In some parts of the world, symptoms resembling anorexia occur without any apparent fear of being fat.* **❞**

Women with anorexia may not even be especially prone to over-estimating the size of their bodies. One study comparing anorexic with healthy women of the same height and weight found that both groups overestimated their size by about the same amount. The anorexic women were more anxious about their body shape only because they had unreasonable standards.

Fasting and Religion

In some parts of the world, symptoms resembling anorexia occur without any apparent fear of being fat. Anorexic women in Hong Kong may say that they have family problems, their appetite is poor, or they simply don't know why they can't eat. In Ghana, women with anorexic symptoms often say they are fasting for religious reasons.

In medieval Europe, for some centuries, fasting almost unto death was regarded as a sign of holiness—a withdrawal from the world and the flesh. One famous medieval ascetic was St. Catherine of Siena, who died at age 32 in 1379, apparently from the effects of starvation. She wrote, "Make a supreme effort to root out that self-love from your heart and to plant in its place this holy self-hatred. This is the royal road by which we turn our back on mediocrity and which leads us without fail to the summit of perfection."

Today's anorexic girls and young women often confess similar thoughts of self-denial and self-perfection. The American Psychiatric Association now classifies a condition with all the symptoms of anorexia nervosa except an obsession with body shape or size as an example of an "eating disorder not otherwise specified."

It's possible that cultures supply only the justification for self-starvation rather than its cause. Some feminists have proposed that women who refuse to eat are misguided rebels making an inarticulate social protest. By refusing to develop a woman's body, they are rejecting a woman's place, whatever that may be in a given culture. Their refusal to eat is a way to show that they are exceptional. How they describe what they are doing—dieting to become thin or fasting to become holy, for example—may depend on the social pressures and opportunities they face.

2

The Signs of Anorexia

Roberto Eguia and Alicia Bello

Roberto Eguia and Alicia Bello are members of the Argentine Asociacion de Lucha Contra Bulimia y Anorexia (the Argentine Association to Fight Bulimia and Anorexia).

Anorexia is appearing with increasing frequency among adolescents of both sexes. Effective treatment often depends on early detection of anorexia symptoms. This is usually difficult, however, because anorexia sufferers try to hide the behaviors typically associated with their disorder. Because of the amount of time they spend with young people, parents and teachers are in the best position to detect the beginning symptoms of anorexia, which often include skipping meals and snacks at school and at home, excessive physical exercise, perfectionism, personality changes, feelings of shame about their bodies, and self-induced vomiting.

Thirty years ago, there was no record of anorexia nervosa and bulimia anywhere in the world. Not because physicians and psychiatrists lacked the tools to detect these disorders, but because the boom of waif-like thinness had not yet invaded western women's collective imagination.

Until the 1960s when Twiggy's skeletal figure traipsed down the catwalk, fashion's spotlight illuminated voluptuous bodies, with the odd little bulge tucked away here and there. Today, however, eating disorders are appearing with an alarming and increasing frequency among adolescents who are obsessed with achieving the "physical ideal." Anorexia and bulimia are appearing at increasingly younger ages and among both sexes (young men currently account for 10% of those suffering from eating disorders).

Thinness is associated with success, power, beauty and status. No wonder "miracle" diets seem a sure way to triumph. These obsessions can lead to serious illness, such as anorexia nervosa, characterized by exaggerated weight loss, or bulimia, in which episodes of bingeing (ingesting large amounts of food) alternate with "compensatory" behavior (such as self-induced vomiting, abuse of laxatives, diuretics, anorexic agents or excessive physical activity).

According to the World Health Organization the mortality rate among those diagnosed with anorexia is 15%.

> *Eating disorders are appearing with an alarming and increasing frequency among adolescents who are obsessed with achieving the 'physical ideal.'*

Argentina's ALUBA (Asociacion de Lucha contra Bulimia y Anorexia, Association to Fight Bulimia and Anorexia) is a non-governmental organization founded and directed by Dr. Mabel Belle. For the past fifteen years, ALUBA has been recognized as a pioneer and leader in the field of eating disorders in Argentina and abroad. Since its creation, ALUBA has handled over 9,000 consultations. Currently, the organization is treating some 2,500 patients and has a high rate of success with a variety of treatment approaches.

In addition to recovery treatments, ALUBA focuses on prevention, early detection and health education. In the schools, ALUBA's activities focus on the population at risk through consciousness-raising initiatives with teachers and parents. Special programs—group discussions, seminars and workshops—train families to prevent anorexia and bulimia and to detect symptoms of eating disorders early on, so that sufferers can receive prompt treatment.

Teachers Are Key

Because teachers are key to identifying pathological behavior in the school setting, ALUBA trains teachers through a specially-designed course in early detection.

The family is the focus of "health education" programs

which emphasize the importance of healthy relationships among family members. Order and mutual respect are prioritized, as are clear, well-defined roles within the family.

Many businesses dedicate time and resources to employees' family welfare, and ALUBA offers these companies prevention programs similar to those offered in the schools. Special explanatory pamphlets, videos and educational materials have been prepared for these activities.

While anorexia nervosa and bulimia are difficult to detect because those who suffer from eating disorders refuse to recognize that they are ill and hide their symptoms. The following are some danger signals.

If parents observe several of these characteristics in a child, a diagnostic consultation may be in order.

In the schools, teachers should take an interest in the issue and collaborate with the families in early detection. Their role is fundamental in the formation of young people free from addictions and prepared to face the challenges of life. For this reason, teachers must be properly informed about eating disorders. If we are able to train them, we strengthen the action of the family in the daily struggle against this scourge. We must therefore re-evaluate the role of teachers in prevention and early detection.

The following are some aspects to which teachers should be attentive:

Eating During Recess

Recess is a break to allow the students to rest and recover their energies in order to continue their activities. During this time to "recharge their batteries," students should eat appropriate food that assures their normal growth and good scholastic performance. The first red light for eating disorders among students is inappropriate eating habits during recess.

Physical Activity and Sports

Encouraging physical activity is healthy, but care should be taken: hyperactivity is one of the symptoms of an eating disorder. When exercise is practiced for the sole purpose of losing weight, in an intense and compulsive fashion and in prolonged sessions, this physical activity is not beneficial but rather activates the illness.

Perfectionism

We pay attention to exemplary students. We admire their work, their dedication to their studies, their habits. They are an example for the rest of the class. But when perfectionism is evident at every moment, this is characteristic of individuals suffering from anorexia.

Teachers should ask themselves: Are they obsessive about their physical appearance? Do they take great pains to have a "perfect" body? What are their eating habits? What are their physical activities?

Changes in Personality

Individuals with eating disorders display aggressive behavior, rage, crying jags, mood swings and withdrawal. If we notice these changes, we should look for other symptoms.

"Ugly Duckling Syndrome"

Low self-esteem and lack of faith in one's ability to succeed lead adolescents to see themselves as "losers." This "ugly duckling syndrome" is characteristic of both anorexia nervosa and bulimia.

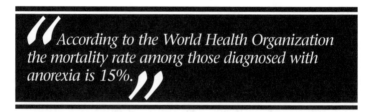

According to the World Health Organization the mortality rate among those diagnosed with anorexia is 15%.

Let's prevent the appearance of eating disorders. Let's encourage students to believe in themselves. Let's teach them to trust in their own abilities.

Values

Our culture admires power, money and the body beautiful above other values that are gradually being lost. If we stop to listen to students' conversations, we hear talk of "miracle diets" or "a great way to lose weight." We should encourage them to focus on other interests, providing an incentive to change and to abandon the fight for the "physical ideal."

Lack of Concentration

Occasionally the performance of a good student may waver; they can't seem to concentrate; and sometimes appear to drift off. Anorexia nervosa and bulimia lock their victims into a minute world in which the only things that matter are weight, calories, the scale and the diet; there is no room for other projects and interests.

Feeling Ashamed of Their Bodies

Because of their distorted body image, students who suffer eating disorders see themselves as "fat" even though they may be a normal weight or even under-weight. They generally try to hide their bodies, to escape the observation of others. They hide in oversized clothes; they refuse to use bathing suits; and they avoid any situations that would force them to show themselves.

Bathroom Use

Among the various methods for eliminating food, self-induced vomiting is one of the most frequent. Special attention should be paid to this behavior, especially after students eat during recess.

Teachers should observe this sort of behavior very carefully because the consequences of self-induced vomiting are very serious. Vomiting can cause decreased levels of potassium in the blood, which can cause heart attacks.

Teachers who become aware of this issue, understand it and collaborate in prevention and early detection of anorexia nervosa and bulimia in the schools are our strongest allies in the struggle against these terrible disorders.

Profile of the Anorexic Patient

• Lack of awareness of the illness
• Intense fear of obesity
• Distorted self-image (they see themselves as fat even though they are under-weight)
• Refusal to maintain normal weight
• Hair loss
• Amenorrhea (lack of menstruation)
• Dry skin
• Hypertension
• Hypothermia

- Habit of cutting food in small bites
- Tendency to eat slowly
- Tendency to chew for a long time
- Preference for small portions
- Habit of spitting out, throwing away or hiding food
- Use of anorexic agents, laxatives and/or diuretics
- Habitual calorie counting
- Rituals revolving around food
- Hyper-activity to lose weight
- Social isolation
- Irritability
- Depression (present in 40–45% of all cases)
- Obsessive behavior
- High demand placed on self
- Rejection of sexuality
- Bingeing
- Use of loose clothing (which hides body)

3

Experiences of a Female Anorexic

Christy Heitger-Casbon

Christy Heitger-Casbon is a writer and editor for Serve, a regional educational laboratory that works to improve learning opportunities for all students. She is also a freelance writer on health and fitness, adolescence, and women's issues.

Some young girls believe that being thin is the key to beauty and popularity. I began to starve myself when I was a young girl in an effort to lose weight and gain friends. Unfortunately, my obsessive desire for thinness triggered anorexia. I was hospitalized until I began to eat again, and I started to recover. The feelings behind my anorexia led me to engage in other obsessive behaviors, however, such as excessive exercising. I have recovered from anorexia and compulsive exercising, but I must remain alert to the start of obsessive behaviors if I am to maintain a healthy lifestyle.

A healthy, balanced, satisfying life is what we all want, isn't it? We bone up on the latest research about nutrition and fitness, buy top-of-the-line health products and exercise equipment and attend the best time management seminars all in hopes of becoming the best we can be. Most of us have such wholesome, sincere, unadulterated intentions. Carrying them out in a healthy manner, however, is a different story. It's often not for lack of trying. It's quite the opposite, actually.

There are those of us who go to extremes in an intense effort to achieve the pinnacle of health. However, when you take things to the extreme, that is precisely when you get yourself

Christy Heitger-Casbon, "Back from the Brink," *American Fitness*, vol. 18, March 2000, p. 32. Copyright © 2000 by the Aerobics and Fitness Association of America. Reproduced by permission of the author.

into trouble. If you eat too much or too little, you feel ill. If you sleep too much or too little, you feel sluggish, if you exercise too much or too little, you harm your body both physically and psychologically. I know because I used to be one of those determined people who took things to the extreme. I still advocate exercise and nutrition, but I don't go overboard anymore because I learned the "lesson of moderation" the hard way.

My Anorexic Nightmare

My story began 14 years ago, when I was 12 years old. I was an awkward middle-schooler who desperately wanted to be beautiful and ached to be popular. It was clear from environmental influences (e.g., peers family and media) that obesity was not acceptable. I heard enough derogatory "fat" comments and witnessed enough pointed fingers while growing up to know that I didn't ever want to be shunned and ridiculed like that. Therefore, I came to the conclusion that to be beautiful and popular, you needed to be thin. Consequently, I started dieting, but I took it to the extreme. Within a three-month period, I had developed anorexia nervosa (a disorder characterized by a preoccupation with thinness and an extremely restrictive diet). Over the course of the summer, I dropped from 110 pounds to a skeletal 73 pounds.

> *I came to the conclusion that to be beautiful and popular, you needed to be thin.*

It's hard to believe that at the tender age of 12 I had already headed down a destructive, devastating and addictive path. People may not think of anorexia as an addiction, but in many ways it is. Experts maintain that all addictions are the pursuit or avoidance of a feeling. As a teenager, I wanted to avoid feeling self-hatred and disgust. I grew tired of looking at myself and being repulsed by what I saw in the mirror, so I starved myself in an attempt to drop pounds and pick up friends. I convinced myself that if I were thin, I'd be accepted and liked by those around me. My ambition backfired, however. Instead of gaining a social network of friends, I landed in an isolated hospital room. Instead of feeling thin, beautiful and popular, I felt grotesque, awkward and lonely. Over the course of the next few years, I received therapy. Throughout my teenage years, I slowly gained weight—ounce by ounce, pound by pound. Three years later, I had returned to a healthy weight. Of course, that didn't mean I had fully recovered psychologically. I still had very low self-confidence, and building that would take a long time.

Running for My Life

I needed to find a way to feel good about myself without falling back into the starvation pattern again, but I didn't quite know how to do that. I started by turning my attention toward something positive rather than negative, focusing on my health rather than my weight. For years, I'd been so preoccupied with the numbers on the scale, I couldn't move beyond that. I wanted to find a way to eat without being terrified of getting fat. Needless to say, this process was arduous and frustrating. For one thing, starving myself for so long had royally screwed up my metabolism. Therefore, I couldn't eat as much as the average woman because my metabolism was so slow. I wanted to find a safe way to give it a boost. I'd read about how exercise helps maintain muscle mass and how this conservation of muscle is important in maintaining a normal metabolic rate. Therefore, I decided to give exercise a try.

I can still recall the first half-mile loop around my neighborhood. Boy, was I pathetic. I was a determined teenager, though, and vowed to persevere. For weeks, I huffed and puffed and absolutely hated lacing up my shoes for my two-mile run. One day, about six months later, I realized, "Hey, I'm actually enjoying this!" Before I knew it, an enthusiastic runner was born.

> *People may not think of anorexia as an addiction, but in many ways it is.*

Running produced a wide range of physical and psychological benefits. Sometimes, I'd catch myself thinking, "Wow, who knew that I could find a fun activity that actually reduces my risk of heart disease and osteoporosis?" I also periodically took my resting heart rate when I first woke up in the morning because I found it amusing to count my heartbeats and knew that as I continued to condition my body, my heart muscle was getting stronger, as were other parts of my body. My lung capacity increased and even the steepest hills didn't leave me breathless anymore. One of the best things ever—especially from a former anorexic's point of view—was to look in a mirror at the body I had loathed for so many years and be able to recognize that it had blossomed into a strong, muscular, curvaceous one. Running definitely gave me the gift of life. Three years ago, however, I began abusing that gift when I started exercising compulsively.

A Few Just Wouldn't Do

When I had anorexia, I found that the more I limited my food intake, the better I felt. This may sound strange, but studies have shown starvation actually alters brain chemistry. Under-eating can activate brain chemicals that produce feelings of peace and euphoria. Some researchers believe that anorexics use the restriction of food to self-medicate painful feelings and distressing moods.

> *Under-eating can activate brain chemicals that produce feelings of peace and euphoria.*

Years later, I subconsciously did the same thing running. I relied on my workouts to suppress and alter my negative emotions. When I first began running, I ran four or five days a week and jogged approximately 20 miles weekly. For seven years, I slowly increased my mileage but still maintained a safe, normal, healthy exercise regimen. It was only when I became addicted to exercise that my behavior turned unhealthy.

I first realized I had a problem when one day, three years ago, I freaked out at the prospect of taking a day off from exercise. My husband and I were in Indiana over Christmas break and a blizzard hit town. Even after the storm subsided, I couldn't run outside because there was blowing and drifting snow. I couldn't get to a gym, either, because the roads were closed. On top of that, my in-laws didn't own a treadmill. When I realized that I had no way of exercising that day, I flipped out. My mind was racing as I desperately tried to figure out an alternative way to run. When I couldn't find a solution, I was overcome by a paralyzing fear. It was so surreal.

> **//** *When I had anorexia, I was actively denying my body's essential nutrients, thereby placing my vital organs . . . at constant risk of failure.* **//**

I thought to myself, "Taking a day off is something I used to do and was fine with. Why does it terrify me now? And what am I afraid of, anyway?" I couldn't explain or rationalize my emotions. All I knew was that I felt completely trapped and amazingly anxious—feelings that only increased with time. In the height of my compulsive exercise addiction, I painstakingly scheduled business meetings and personal vacations around my running regimen. In 1995, I even scheduled the time of my wedding around my daily run. I knew this wasn't normal, yet I couldn't change my behavior.

Risky Business

My running routine didn't become a problem until I let it consume and control me. Just as my moderate exercise routine had originally produced numerous benefits, my excessive running routine produced numerous problems. I experienced knee pain, hip pain, ankle pain, muscle cramps, headaches, shin splints and pulled muscles, but the discomfort was never enough to prompt me to cut back on my workouts. Despite the fact these pains were a direct result of my compulsive running, I chose to overlook the adverse consequences and continued to run. . . .

When I had anorexia, I was actively denying my body's essential nutrients, thereby placing my vital organs (i.e., heart, lungs, kidneys) at constant risk of failure. However, no matter the risks, I stubbornly refused to eat. I understood I needed to gain weight to stay alive, but found the actual process of lifting food to my lips too much to bear. Ultimately, I couldn't, wouldn't and didn't eat until I was hospitalized and forced to do so.

Everyone knows that excessively limiting food intake is dangerous, but recognizing excessive exercise as dangerous isn't quite as obvious because the signs aren't visible or evident. Nevertheless, the danger is just as real. Just as my old addiction had a name (anorexia), my new one did, too. Researchers call it "anorexia athletica" or "compulsive exercise," and its consequences are numerous. Anorexia Nervosa and Related Eating Disorders (ANRED) reports that the consequences of compulsive exercise include abandoned relationships, damaged careers, lower grades in school, stress fractures, as well as damaged bones, joints, and soft tissues. Some psychological effects include obsessive thoughts, compulsive behaviors, self-worth measured only in terms of performance, depression, guilt and anxiety when exercise is impossible. . . .

> *Ultimately, I couldn't, wouldn't and didn't eat until I was hospitalized and forced to do so.*

Six months ago, after concluding that I wanted to be an "avid" runner rather than an "addicted" one, I altered my exercise regimen. I began by slowly reducing my mileage and adding cross-training activities such as weightlifting, biking, swimming and tennis. Then, I started taking two "rest" days a week. Admittedly, allowing myself rest days was not easy to do. As strange as it sounds, for a while, I felt guilty for getting hungry on days I hadn't exercised. My first inclination was to cut back on my food intake on my rest days. Nancy Clark, M.S., R.D., author of *Nancy Clark's Sports Nutrition Guidebook*, warns against this because, as she says, "Your muscles will be busy replacing glycogen stores with the carbohydrates you normally burn off during exercise."

I've actually grown to appreciate my rest days because I don't view them as lazy, inactive days, but rather as free, unstructured ones. On these days, I'll take long evening walks with my husband or swim a few easy laps in the pool to unwind. It just depends on what I feel like doing.

Psychological and Physical Benefits

I've noticed both psychological and physical benefits as a result of my new, balanced approach to health and fitness. Psychologically, I feel much healthier since I began exercising in moderation. Now that every second of my day doesn't revolve around my workout, I enjoy life more. I know that I'll get my workout in because I'm still an enthusiastic and motivated individual, but I don't let obsessive thoughts about exercise consume me anymore. For example, if something comes up and I have to push my workout back a couple of hours, it's not a big deal. (I couldn't have said that a year ago.) . . .

I've lived so much of my life in fear of things—fear of getting fat, fear of losing control, fear of what others think of me, fear of failure and fear of disappointing others. However, I've let go of all that. Fear and obsession no longer rule my life. I'm finally living a healthy, sensible and balanced lifestyle.

4
Experiences of a Male Anorexic

Thomas Holbrook

Thomas Holbrook is a psychiatrist and clinical director of the Eating Disorders Program at Rogers Memorial Hospital in Oconomowoc, Wisconsin.

My eating disorder began when I had to stop running due to knee problems. I started obsessing about my weight—afraid that I would get fat since I was no longer engaged in strenuous exercise—and began cutting calories. Over a ten year period, I slipped deeper into anorexia and was hospitalized several times. No one ever questioned my eating habits or diagnosed my anorexia. I believe that this is because I am a man and anorexia is associated with women. Ultimately, I diagnosed myself and began treatment. Even then, many of my colleagues had difficulty believing that I—a man—was anorexic. After extensive therapy, I have successfully recovered from anorexia.

In the spring of 1976, two years into my psychiatric practice, I began having pain in both knees, which soon severely limited my running. I was advised by an orthopedist to stop trying to run through the pain. After many failed attempts to treat the condition with orthotic surgery and physical therapy, I resigned myself to giving up running. As soon as I made that decision, the fear of gaining weight and getting fat consumed me. I started weighing myself every day, and even though I was not gaining weight, I started feeling fatter. I became increasingly obsessed about my energy balance and whether I was burning off the calories I consumed. I refined my knowledge of nutrition and memorized the calories and grams of fat, protein, and carbohydrates of every food I would possibly eat.

Despite what my intellect told me, my goal became to rid my body of all fat. I resumed exercising. I found I could walk good distances, despite some discomfort, if I iced my knees afterward. I started walking several times a day. I built a small pool in my basement and swam in place, tethered to the wall. I biked as much as I could tolerate. The denial of what I only much later came to recognize as anorexia involved overuse injuries as I sought medical help for tendonitis, muscle and joint pain, and entrapment neuropathies. I was never told that I was exercising too much, but I am sure that had I been told, I would not have listened.

Worst Nightmare

Despite my efforts, my worst nightmare was happening. I felt and saw myself as fatter than ever before, even though I had started to lose weight. Whatever I had learned about nutrition in medical school or read in books, I perverted to my purpose. I obsessed about protein and fat. I increased the number of egg whites that I ate a day to 12. If any yolk leaked into my concoction of egg whites, Carnation Instant Breakfast, and skim milk, I threw the entire thing out.

As I became more restrictive, caffeine became more and more important and functional for me. It staved off my appetite, although I didn't let myself think about it that way. Coffee and soda perked me up emotionally and focused my thinking. I really do not believe that I could have continued to function at work without caffeine.

> **//** *Despite what my intellect told me, my goal became to rid my body of all fat.* **//**

I relied equally on my walking (up to six hours a day) and restrictive eating to fight fat, but it seemed I could never walk far enough or eat little enough. The scale was now the final analysis of everything about me. I weighed myself before and after every meal and walk. An increase in weight meant I had not tried hard enough and needed to walk farther or on steeper hills, and eat less. If I lost weight, I was encouraged and all the more determined to eat less and exercise more. However, my goal was not to be thinner, just not fat. I still wanted to be "big and strong"—just not fat.

Ritualistic Eating

Besides the scale, I measured myself constantly by assessing how my clothes fit and felt on my body. I compared myself to other people, using this information to "keep me on track." As I had when I compared myself to others in terms of intelligence, talent, humor, and personality, I fell short in all categories. All of those feelings were channeled into the final "fat equation."

> **// Whatever I had learned about nutrition in medical school or read in books, I perverted to my purpose. //**

During the last few years of my illness, my eating became more extreme. My meals were extremely ritualistic, and by the time I was ready for dinner, I had not eaten all day and had exercised five or six hours. My suppers became a relative binge. I still thought of them as "salads," which satisfied my anorexic mind. They evolved from just a few different types of lettuce and some raw vegetables and lemon juice for dressing to rather elaborate concoctions. I must have been at least partly aware that my muscles were wasting away because I made a point of adding protein, usually in the form of tuna fish. I added other foods from time to time in a calculated and compulsive way. Whatever I added, I had to continue with, and usually in increasing amounts. A typical binge might consist of a head of iceberg lettuce, a full head of raw cabbage, a defrosted package of frozen spinach, a can of tuna, garbanzo beans, croutons, sunflower seeds, artificial bacon bits, a can of pineapple, lemon juice, and vinegar, all in a foot-and-a-half-wide bowl. In my phase of eating carrots, I would eat about a pound of raw carrots while I was preparing the salad. The raw cabbage was my laxative. I counted on that control over my bowels for added reassurance that the food was not staying in my body long enough to make me fat.

The final part of my ritual was a glass of cream sherry. Although I obsessed all day about my binge, I came to depend on the relaxing effect of the sherry. My long-standing insomia worsened as my eating became more disordered, and I became dependent on the soporific effect of alcohol. When I was not in too much physical discomfort from the binge, the food and alcohol would put me to sleep, but only for about four hours or so. I awoke at 2:30 or 3:00 A.M. and started my walks. It was always in the back of my mind that I would not be accruing fat if I wasn't sleeping. And, of course, moving was always better than not. Fatigue also helped me modify the constant anxiety I felt. Over-the-counter cold medications, muscle relaxants, and Valium also gave me relief from my anxiety. The combined effect of medication with low blood sugar was relative euphoria.

Oblivious to Illness

While I was living this crazy life, I was carrying on my psychiatric practice, much of which consisted of treating eating-disordered patients—anorexic, bulimic, and obese. It is incredible to me now that I could be working with anorexic patients who were not any sicker than I was, even healthier in some ways, and yet remain completely oblivious to my own illness. There were only extremely brief flashes of insight. If I happened to see myself in a mirrored window reflection, I would be horrified at how emaciated I appeared. Turning away, the insight was gone. I was well aware of my usual self-doubts and insecurities, but that was normal for me. Unfortunately, the increasing spaciness that I was experiencing with weight loss and minimal nutrition was also becoming "normal" for me. In fact, when I was at my spaciest, I felt the best, because it meant that I was not getting fat.

> *The scale was now the final analysis of everything about me.*

Only occasionally would a patient comment on my appearance. I would blush, feel hot, and sweat with shame but not recognize cognitively what he or she was saying. More surprising to me, in retrospect, was never having been confronted about my eating or weight loss by the professionals with whom I worked all during this time. I remember a physician administrator of the hospital kidding me occasionally about eating so little, but I was never seriously questioned about my eating, weight loss, or exercise. They all must have seen me out walking for an hour or two every day regardless of the weather. I even had a down-filled body suit that I would put over my work clothes, allowing me to walk no matter how low the temperature. My work must have suffered during these years, but I did not notice or hear about it.

> *If I lost weight, I was encouraged and all the more determined to eat less and exercise more.*

People outside of work seemed relatively oblivious as well. Family registered concern about my overall health and the various physical problems I was having but were apparently completely unaware of the connection with my eating and weight loss, poor nutrition, and excessive exercise. I was never exactly gregarious, but my social isolation became extreme in my illness. I declined social invitations as much as I could. This included family gatherings. If I accepted an invitation that would include a meal, I would either not eat or bring my own food. During those years, I was virtually friendless.

ER Visits Yield No Diagnosis

I still find it hard to believe that I was so blind to the illness, especially as a physician aware of the symptoms of anorexia nervosa. I could see my weight dropping but could only believe it was good, despite conflicting thoughts about it. Even when I started feeling weak and tired, I did not understand. As I experienced the progressive physical sequelae of my weight loss, the picture only grew murkier. My bowels stopped functioning normally, and I developed severe abdominal cramping and diarrhea. In addition to the cabbage, I was sucking on packs of sugarless candies, sweetened with Sorbitol to diminish hunger and for its laxative effect. At my worst, I was spending up to a couple of hours a day in the bathroom. In the winter I had severe Raynaud's Phenomenon, during which all the digits on my hands and feet would become white and excruciatingly painful. I was dizzy and lightheaded. Severe back spasms occurred occasionally, resulting in a number of ER visits by ambulance. I was asked no questions and no diagnosis was made despite my physical appearance and low vital signs.

Around this time I was recording my pulse down into the 30s. I remember thinking that this was good because it meant that I was "in shape." My skin was paper thin. I became increasingly tired during the day and would find myself almost dozing off while in sessions with patients. I was short of breath at times and would feel my heart pound. One night I was shocked to discover that I had pitting edema of both legs up to my knees. Also around that time, I fell while ice skating and bruised my knee. The swelling was enough to tip the cardiac balance, and I passed out. More trips to the ER and several admissions to the hospital for assessment and stabilization still resulted in no diagnosis. Was it because I was a man?

I was finally referred to the Mayo Clinic with the hope of identifying some explanation for my myriad of symptoms. During the week at Mayo, I saw almost every kind of specialist and was tested exhaustively. However, I was never questioned about my eating or exercise habits. They only remarked that I had an extremely high carotene level and that my skin was certainly orangish (this was during one of my phases of high carrot consumption). I was told that my problems were "functional," or, in other words, "in my head," and that they probably stemmed from my father's suicide 12 years earlier.

Physician, Heal Thyself

An anorexic woman with whom I had been working for a couple of years finally reached me when she questioned whether she could trust me. At the end of a session on a Thursday, she asked for reassurance that I would be back on Monday and continue to work with her. I replied that, of course, I would be back, "I don't abandon my patients."

She said, "My head says yes, but my heart says no." After attempting to reassure her, I did not give it a second thought until Saturday morning, when I heard her words again.

I was staring out my kitchen window, and I started experiencing deep feelings of shame and sadness. For the first time I recognized that I was anorexic, and I was able to make sense of what had happened to me over the last 10 years. I could identify all the symptoms of anorexia that I knew so well in my patients. While this was a relief, it was also very frightening. I felt alone and terrified of what I knew I had to do—let other people know that I was anorexic. I had to eat and stop exercising compulsively. I had no idea if I could really do it—I had been this way for so long. I could not imagine what recovery would be like or how I could possibly be okay without my eating disorder.

> *My social isolation became extreme in my illness.*

I was afraid of the responses that I would get. I was doing individual and group therapy with mostly eating-disordered patients in two inpatient programs, one for young adults (ages 12 to 22) and the other for older adults. For some reason, I was more anxious about the younger group. My fears proved unfounded. When I told them that I was anorexic, they were as accepting and supportive of me and my illness as they were of one another. There was more of a mixed response from hospital staff. One of my colleagues heard about it and suggested that my restrictive eating was merely a "bad habit" and that I could not *really* be anorexic. Some of my coworkers were immediately supportive; others seemed to prefer not to talk about it.

That Saturday I knew what I was facing. I had a fairly good idea of what I would have to change. I had no idea how slow the process would be or how long it would take. With the dropping of my denial, recovery became a possibility and gave me some direction and purpose outside of the structure of my eating disorder.

Supper Was the Easiest Meal

The eating was slow to normalize. It helped to start thinking of eating three meals a day. My body needed more than I could eat in three meals, but it took me a long time to be comfortable eating snacks. Grain, protein, and fruit were the easiest food groups to eat consistently. Fat and dairy groups took much longer to include. Supper continued to be my easiest meal and breakfast came easier than lunch. It helped to eat meals out. I was never really safe just cooking for myself. I started eating breakfast and lunch at the hospital where I worked and eating suppers out.

During my marital separation and for a few years after the divorce from my first wife, my children spent weekdays with their mother and weekends with me. Eating was easier when I was taking care of them because I simply had to have food around for them. I met and courted my second wife during this time, and by the time we were married, my son Ben was in college and my daughter Sarah was applying to go. My second wife enjoyed cooking and would cook supper for us. This was the first time since high school that I had had suppers prepared for me.

After ten years in recovery, my eating now seems second nature to me. Although I still have occasional days of feeling fat and still have a tendency to choose foods lower in fat and calories, eating is relatively easy because I go ahead and eat what I need. During more difficult times I still think of it in terms of what I *need to eat*, and I will even carry on a brief inner dialogue about it.

> ❝ *Several admissions to the hospital . . . still resulted in no diagnosis. Was it because I was a man?* ❞

My second wife and I divorced awhile back, but it is still hard to shop for food and cook by myself. Eating out is safe for me now, however. I will sometimes order the special, or the same selection that someone else is ordering as a way of staying safe and letting go of my control over the food.

Toning Down

While I worked on my eating, I struggled to stop exercising compulsively. This proved much harder to normalize than the eating. Because I was eating more, I had a stronger drive to exercise to cancel calories. But the drive to exercise seemed also to have deeper roots. It was relatively easy to see how including several fats at a meal was something I needed to do to recover from this illness. But it was harder to reason in the same way for exercise. Experts talk about separating it from the illness and somehow preserving it for the obvious benefits of health and enjoyment. Even this is tricky. I enjoy exercise even when I am obviously doing it excessively. . . .

Being Oneself

One of the most significant insights I've gained in my recovery has been that I have spent my whole life trying to be somebody I'm not. Just like so many of my patients, I had the feeling that I was never good enough. In my own estimation, I was a failure. Any compliments or recognition of achievement did not fit. On the contrary, I always expected to be "found out"—that others would discover that I was stupid, and it would be all over. Always starting with the premise that who I am is not good enough, I have gone to such extremes to improve what I assumed needed improvement. My eating disorder was one of those extremes. It blunted my anxieties and gave me a false sense of security through the control over food, body shape, and weight. My recovery has allowed me to experience these same anxieties and insecurities without the necessity of escape through control over food. . . .

I have not had to change in the ways that I initially feared. I have let myself respect the interests and feelings that I have always had. I can experience my fears without needing to escape.

5

Anorexia Occurs Among African Americans

Shannah Tharp-Taylor

Shannah Tharp-Taylor is a staff reporter for the Chicago Tribune.

Black women often suffer needlessly from anorexia because doctors do not expect to find eating disorders in the African American community and thus misdiagnose their anorexic patients. It has been thought that the African American community's greater acceptance of larger body sizes for women offers black teens some protection against anorexia. However, as African Americans take on the cultural values of the mainstream—white—culture, any protection provided by greater acceptance of diverse body types has diminished. While more research on eating disorders in minorities is needed, it appears that anorexia depends more on socioeconomic status than on race.

In many ways, Stephanie Doswell is your regular college student in a T-shirt and flare-legged jeans. But she is also anorexic, bulimic and African-American, a combination so rare that it sometimes goes unrecognized.

"If someone sees a sickly, thin white person, they automatically think that they have anorexia," said Doswell, 19. "If someone sees a sickly, thin black person, they don't think that they have anorexia."

She adds sarcastically: "Because blacks don't get anorexia."

While their numbers are probably small, black anorexics face a host of unique problems, including inadequate diag-

Shannah Tharp-Taylor, "Anorexia Among Black Women Gets New Scrutiny," *Chicago Tribune*, August 25, 2003, p. 1. Copyright © 2003 by the *Chicago Tribune*. Reproduced by permission.

noses from doctors not expecting to find eating disorders in African-Americans.

Anorexia has been thought of as a disease affecting rich, white females since the 1940s because it primarily affects girls from well-to-do Caucasian families.

Recent studies seem to confirm that black anorexics are extremely hard to find. Last month [July 2003] Ruth Striegel-Moore of Wesleyan University in Connecticut reported in the *American Journal of Psychiatry* that although anorexia is believed to affect 1 percent to 2 percent of the general population, none of the 1,061 young black women in their study was anorexic.

But many experts doubt that black anorexics are as rare as studies have suggested, though experts are left guessing at how prevalent the disease is in minorities.

Traditionally, African-American girls have been thought to have some protection from eating disorders such as anorexia nervosa and bulimia nervosa because of a greater acceptance of larger body size in the African-American community, said Gayle Brooks, an African-American psychologist specializing in eating disorders at the Renfrew Center in Florida.

Gaps in Knowledge

But this alleged protection from eating disorders appears to weaken as blacks take on the values of the mainstream culture, Brooks says.

"I think that there are a lot of African-American women who are really struggling with their sense of personal identity and self-esteem that comes with being a part of this culture that does not accept who we really are," Brooks said.

> *Black anorexics face a host of unique problems, including inadequate diagnoses from doctors not expecting to find eating disorders in African-Americans.*

For years anorexia (characterized by refusal to eat enough) and bulimia (characterized by binge eating and purging) was only studied in white females, leaving gaps in medical knowledge about eating disorders and how they affect minorities.

For example, experts are not sure whether black girls from high-income families are more likely than their poorer counterparts to develop eating disorders, as is believed to be the case for white girls.

Striegel-Moore acknowledges that her study may have underestimated the number of blacks with anorexia nervosa because she had too few girls from affluent black families.

> **⁣⁣*Many experts doubt that black anorexics are as rare as studies have suggested.*⁣⁣**

Similarly, psychologists typically search for anorexia in adolescents, the age group commonly found to have the disorder in white girls. However, experts question whether anorexia may develop later in African-Americans.

Thomas Joiner, a professor of psychology at Florida State University, tested whether racial stereotypes influence the recognition of eating disorders. He asked 150 people to read a fictional diary of a 16-year-old girl named Mary and rated whether they thought the girl had an eating disorder.

For some the diary was labeled "Mary, 16-year-old Caucasian." For others it was labeled "Mary, 16-year-old African-American."

More people said the subject had an eating disorder when she was labeled white than when she was labeled black.

"Race mattered," Joiner said. "There's the idea in people's minds that African-American girls tend not to get eating disorders. And that influenced their judgments."

Joiner and his colleagues also found that many health care professionals were unable to recognize black anorexics, suggesting that could contribute to missed diagnoses.

"(Doctors) should have their same radar out for eating disorders when talking with an African-American girl as when they are sitting across from Caucasian girls," Joiner said.

One 17-year-old African-American girl from Washington, D.C., said her doctors did not diagnose her properly, even though she has been purging since age 10 and at 5 foot 7 has weighed as little as 95 pounds.

"The doctors just thought I had a stomach thing. . . . They gave me antibiotics and rehydrated me and sent me home," said the girl, who replied to an e-mail request from the *Chicago Tribune* asking African-American anorexics to share their stories.

One's Social Group Is More Important than One's Race

Many researchers and clinicians studying anorexia nervosa say that becoming anorexic is less a factor of race and more a consideration of one's social group.

However, girls from poor families face an additional risk because they are not likely to be able to afford treatment, which can cost as much as $30,000 for a month of in-patient care.

Doswell typifies some of the issues surrounding anorexia in black women.

Her condition was verified through her therapist, Keitha Austin of Newport News, Va., who received written permission to confirm that Doswell is an African-American female with anorexia.

She starts each day with eight melon-flavored gummy rings.

"I don't want a booty like J. Lo, [Jennifer Lopez, a Latina pop star]" Doswell said. "I don't want to look like Beyonce [an African-American pop star] because she is fat."

> *African-American girls have been thought to have . . . protection from eating disorders . . . because of a greater acceptance of larger body sizes in the African-American community.*

Holidays at the Doswell home are filled with soul food, Doswell wrote in an e-mail interview. "Catfish, beans, collard greens. . . . Food is important to us," said Doswell, who describes her family as lower-middle class.

At 5 feet 4 inches tall—about average—Doswell weighs 93 pounds, less than 97 percent of women her age. She wears a size 3, she says, because she likes her clothes baggy.

Doswell said she envied her white, Hispanic and Asian friends, who were thin and preoccupied with weight.

Her roller coaster with eating disorders began in anticipation of an exchange program trip to Japan.

"I didn't want to be fat on the trip," Doswell said. "So, I

just stopped eating. It was that simple."

Thirteen pounds later, Doswell was still not happy with her new, thinner self. So she forced her weight lower into the upper 90s.

By spring 2002 she was eating only rice or fruit and exercising incessantly, stealing laxatives and throwing up the little food she consumed. But she did not know that her behaviors had a name.

> **❝** *Many health care professionals were unable to recognize black anorexics.* **❞**

"I went online one day and found out that what I was doing was actually a disease," she said.

The Web has become a haven for young women with eating disorders who feel they have nowhere else to turn for help and support. The issue of race and stereotypes about eating disorders are hot topics for members of the Colours of Ana Web site, created as a support system for girls and women of color with anorexia and other eating disorders.

Many girls on the www.coloursofana.com site wrote that they have heard negative comments from other blacks suggesting that they developed anorexia because they are trying to be white by becoming thin.

"I have an eating disorder because I am sick, not because I am wanting to be white," wrote one woman. "We need to get past this sort of exclusivity. It is just not helping."

Race Is No Protection from Anorexia

In the mid-'80s Zina Garrison, a professional tennis star, looked around the tennis world and did not see anyone who looked like her.

"I didn't really have anyone to look up to," Garrison said in an interview. "At the time it was basically myself, Jackie Joyner-Kersee and Florence Joyner who were the pivotal African-American women athletes doing something."

At 21 years old, Garrison was ranked in the top 10 of women's tennis and had beaten Chris Evert. But still she struggled with self-image.

"I was in a short skirt all of the time, and I was always told that I didn't have the figure to fit the tennis skirts," Garrison said.

In an effort to fit the mold of the all-white world of women's tennis and the emptiness she felt as an athlete and public figure, Garrison tumbled into bulimic behavior without actually knowing that she was developing an eating disorder.

Purging took a toll on Garrison's health. Her hair started to fall out. Her skin became blotchy. Her nails softened.

Garrison became too weak to play the game she loved.

After watching a television show on bulimia and eating disorders, Garrison recognized her behavior as an illness, got help from her trainers and went on to return to the top of the tennis world as a winner of major tournaments.

Even now, Garrison said, "Recovery goes on day by day."

Kaelyn Carson was not as fortunate.

At 5 foot 8 and 115 pounds of solid muscle, Kaelyn Carson, of Comstock Park, Mich., was a brown-eyed beauty with long, curly brown hair and big dimples. But after a 14-month battle with anorexia and bulimia, Carson died at age 20. She weighed 75 pounds.

Carson, who was biracial—African American and white—exemplifies the fact that no one is immune from eating disorders because of her race.

"She was everything," said her mother, Brenda Carson.

But now she is left with only memories of her daughter, who was a member of the National Association of Collegiate Scholars, Miss Michigan American Teen, a cheerleader and a track star.

"Don't close your eyes to it," her mother said.

6

Anorexia Can Strike Older Women

Sabrina Rubin Erdely

Sabrina Rubin Erdely is a nationally known freelance writer whose work has appeared in many publications including Philadelphia Magazine, Glamour, *and* Redbook.

While the majority of Americans who suffer from eating disorders are under age twenty-five, an increasing number of women in their thirties and older are showing symptoms of anorexia. Psychiatrists maintain that the sources of stress in an adult woman's life are different—marriage, children, job—from that of a teen, but the response is the same: acute anxiety and stress. Thus, older women and teens both become anorexic in a misguided attempt to cope with stress and take control of a life that seems wildly out of control. Recovery from anorexia is often more difficult for adults than for teens, however, because most adults have responsibilities that cannot easily be put aside while they spend time in treatment centers. Also, adults must often return to the same stressful situations that triggered their anorexia. Learning new ways of coping with stress is the key to long-term adult recovery from anorexia.

Kathy Palmero woke up in the back of an ambulance. Foggily she tried to recall how she had gotten there. She lifted her head from the stretcher to look down at herself, at her thin body dressed in a too-big pantsuit. Oh, right. It was all coming back to her now. The 31-year-old sales executive had just returned to work after her lunch break. She had been sitting at her desk, chatting with a coworker. Then everything had gone black: Kathy had passed out cold. The embarrassing incident was just one more sign, Kathy felt, that her life was spinning out of control. The Pennsylvania resident had two colicky children under the age of 2 at home, who kept her awake all night with their fussing. Kathy's husband, Chris, was a state trooper who worked the night shift, so he couldn't offer her much help on that front. In fact, he and Kathy often saw each other only at dinnertime (Chris' breakfast) before he raced out the door. Worse, Kathy was still in emotional shambles after her mother's death six months before. With a demanding career added to the mix, the pressure had become too much.

> **An increasing number of women in their 30s are also falling prey to eating disorders.**

But in the midst of her private chaos, Kathy had discovered a way of managing her stress: She had all but ceased to eat. It began with fat-free foods and diet soda. Then her portions got smaller—and smaller. As the pounds flew off her five-foot-five, 168-pound frame, Kathy watched with pleasure as her curvy body transformed. Realizing that her rapid weight loss wasn't quite normal or healthy, Kathy never explained her strict regimen to anyone, offering only vague explanations to her friends and family about her increasingly slim physique.

Now, as Kathy's ambulance pulled up to the hospital, she cursed herself for allowing her secret to get out into the open. Sure enough, during a follow-up appointment a week later, Kathy's physician asked her whether she had been eating much. But by then, Kathy had her answer ready.

"Of course," she lied. Since Kathy wasn't drastically thin— at that point she weighed 120 pounds—the doctor believed her and sent her home. My secret's safe, Kathy said to herself with a sigh. Kathy, however, was anything but safe.

The Newest Victims of Eating Disorders

Anorexia and bulimia used to be ailments associated only with turbulent teenage years, and the majority of the five to ten million American sufferers are still under age 25.

But in a new phenomenon noticed by psychiatrists and

treatment centers, an increasing number of women in their 30s are also falling prey to eating disorders. "It's not just a teenage problem anymore," says Samuel E. Menaged, president of the Renfrew Center, the nation's largest eating-disorder facility. In the past, only a sprinkling of women over the age of 30 had sought inpatient help. But when the Renfrew staff looked at its 2003 roster, they realized that nearly a third of their residential patients were in this age group. At least half of them had suffered from eating disorders earlier in life; the other half were brand-new cases. "We're witnessing a very real shift," says William Davis, Ph.D., vice president of research and program development at Renfrew. "It's a trend that I suspect is going to continue to grow."

Whether you're 13 or 30, the main issue behind an eating disorder remains the same: It's a misguided way of coping with stress, a way of imposing control in your otherwise crazy life. But the stresses that can trigger an eating disorder in your 30s are very different from those that teens face. They tend to be uniquely adult concerns, ones that stem from the everyday juggling act of being a wife, a mother, and an employee—things like marital strain, job stress, child-rearing worries, and financial decisions.

> *Whether you're 13 or 30, the main issue behind an eating disorder remains the same: It's a misguided way of coping with stress.*

"Playing all those roles creates anxiety. All that anxiety makes women feel negative about themselves, because women tend to blame themselves instead of blaming the situation," observes Davis. "They can't say, 'I simply don't have time to get things done'; they say, 'What's wrong with me that I can't get things done?'"

And that self-doubt plays itself out against a charged backdrop: the societal pressure to be thin. For a woman in her 30s—who may be having babies, developing her first wrinkles, and noticing her slowing metabolism—it introduces yet another thing to worry about. "Women in our culture are bombarded with the notion that you have to be thin to be OK," says Davis. "So now you have women who are feeling vulnerable or troubled, and they are hitting on thinness as a solution to their problems as well as a sign that they're in charge of their lives."

The Role of Genetics

Of course, not every woman who's on a diet and has too much on her to-do list winds up with an eating disorder. The main factor that determines who's most vulnerable may be genetic: A study at UCLA found that female relatives of women with anorexia or bulimia are up to 12 times more likely to develop an eating disorder than women in unaffected families. Personality also plays a strong role. "Traits like perfectionism, anxiety, and a desire to please others are extremely common among people with eating disorders," adds Davis. That doesn't mean that everybody with such traits gets an eating disorder; it only means that those people, if exposed to a certain environment (for example, one that fosters low self-esteem or poor body image), are more likely to develop one.

> *You have women who are feeling vulnerable or troubled, and they are hitting on thinness as a solution to their problems.*

Many sufferers, like Kathy Palmero, live for months or years in denial that they have an eating disorder. And even when they do realize that they're harming themselves, they tend to cling desperately to the comfort and sense of order that their anorexia or bulimia brings. For harried women who lack precious "me time," eating disorders can also represent something more. Since their activity of paring portions, bingeing and purging, or taking laxatives is something they engage in entirely alone—a private regimen or even a "pleasure" not performed for their husband or kids—they tend to view it as a cherished indulgence, a twisted logic that can make this disorder even harder to overcome.

When a Diet Gets Dangerous

For some women, eating disorders appear seemingly out of nowhere, overwhelming them even if they never had weight issues as a teen. That was definitely the case with Kathy, who dieted occasionally during her youth but never in an unhealthy way. "I was never fat, but I was always big-boned," Kathy says. Outgoing Kathy learned to play her insecurity for laughs each year she'd joke with her future husband, Chris, about how for her birthday she wanted "anorexia, but only for a week." "It was a big standing joke," she remembers.

> *Female relatives of women with anorexia or bulimia are up to 12 times more likely to develop an eating disorder than women in unaffected families.*

Life quickly changed for Kathy at 27, after she married Chris. In rapid succession, she gave birth to her first child and got pregnant again—and spent that pregnancy caring not only for her infant son but also for her 55-year-old mother, who was gravely ill with a brain tumor and died when Kathy was seven months along. Adding to her devastation was the fact that Chris, working odd hours, was almost never around. On top of it all, Kathy's back-to-back pregnancies had saddled her with additional pounds. "You'll never be skinny again, not after two C-sections," one coworker clucked. At 30, Kathy suddenly didn't recognize her life anymore. "Before having kids I would go out to dinner with friends. I had time with my husband, time to myself," she says. "Two years later I woke up and I was a mom, and my life had totally changed. I resented everything."

Kathy started losing weight from the stress, which robbed her of her appetite. Thrilled with the results, Kathy decided to go on a real diet. First she avoided anything with fat, drastically reduced her portion sizes, and hid her skimpy meals from her husband by pushing food around on her plate. Within six months, Kathy lost 80 pounds. Still, she kept at it. "I couldn't do anything about my mother's death, or my husband's job, or the fact that my kids never slept," she says. "But my weight was one thing I could control. And I did it well." At her thinnest, Kathy weighed just 85 pounds.

Her husband was unaware of her problem for months, in part because of their different schedules. One day, however, when Chris caught sight of Kathy in her underwear, he freaked out. "Jesus Christ, what happened to you?" he exclaimed. Kathy made a lot of excuses, and Chris didn't know what to believe— a common mistake among men who aren't taught to recognize the symptoms of an eating disorder. Kathy, in turn, was masterful at hiding her problem, as she had done with her doctor and her coworkers months earlier, when she fainted in her office.

Then one fateful day, Kathy's father came to visit—with his new girlfriend. Still mired in grief over her mother's death less than a year earlier, "that put me over the edge," she says. Overwhelmed with the need to purge, she excused herself to go to the bathroom, where she drank from a bottle of ipecac syrup and dry-heaved until she lost consciousness. Her 1½-year-old son eventually found her limp figure on the bathroom floor and called out for his dad. When Kathy finally awoke in the company of her worried husband and son, she knew she had hit rock bottom and decided to get help: "The fact that my son saw me like that, I thought, 'What the hell are you doing? If you keep this up, you won't be able to be a mother to your kids.'"

When Weight Is a Lifetime Struggle

While some women find themselves struggling with eating disorders for the first time in their lives as adults, for others, it's a more familiar battle: They experience the disorder as teens, then suffer relapses. . . .

> *At first, women with eating disorders often see their slimmer bodies as a sign they've finally taken control of their lives.*

At first, women with eating disorders often see their slimmer bodies as a sign they've finally taken control of their lives. But sooner or later, most come up against the harsh truth: that their disorder controls them, sometimes subtly forcing them to sacrifice the things that they normally hold dear. Janice Fingland, 38, knows this all too well. It started when, while trying to take some weight off her five-foot-one, 178-pound frame, she went on the Atkins diet and took a laxative to relieve her constipation. Thrilled the next day when she had lost two pounds, Janice started popping laxatives daily—and the pounds kept melting away. "I was getting compliments like crazy!" she says. "It was so flattering. I felt like I had finally taken charge of my looks."

Marital Problems

Then Janice began to look starved and unhealthy. Her shoulder blades began looking bony, her neck scrawny. When her second husband, Jeff, became suspicious, Janice broke down and confessed her laxative habit, and promised she would stop using the pills. As soon as she stopped, however, Janice swelled with water retention as her dehydrated body held on to every drop of fluid she consumed. Unable to button her jeans, Janice panicked. "I didn't want to get fat again," she says. Janice threw herself back into her disorder, secretly cutting her daily meal plan down to just one salad—plus 30 laxatives, an all-time high.

> **//**Due to malnutrition, older patients are even more prone to osteoporosis, and may be at a higher risk for . . . heart attack, and even death. **//**

Jeff realized that his wife had returned to her self-destructive habits and researched therapists for her to consult, but she refused to call one. As her weight dropped to 100 pounds, Jeff finally gave Janice an ultimatum. "He was pushing me to get help, and I didn't want to. So we separated," Janice says, sounding as if she can hardly believe it herself. "I chose the laxatives over my own husband." Janice was numb the day Jeff packed and left. He told her that he would return when she decided to seek treatment.

Janice's daughters, then a 13-year-old and 10-year-old twins, were confused about their stepfather's sudden absence and why their mom seemed increasingly removed. She was exhausted, depressed, and sometimes racked with chest pains, which can occur in women with eating disorders. Nine months after Jeff moved out—and after having lived with anorexia for three years—Janice knew she couldn't go on much longer. "I saw my life crumbling before me," she recalls. "I stopped bonding with my kids. I had pushed my husband out of the house and didn't even know why. I knew I wasn't happy. Finally I said, 'I'm done. I need help.'"

She made two calls: one to her therapist and one to her husband, who moved back home a few weeks later, after she showed him that she was serious about beating her disorder. "Jeff had been through Alcoholics Anonymous 15 years before, so he knew that until I was ready to get help, I'd push everybody away," she says. "So he let me go—but also let me know that he'd be there when I was ready to say, 'I can't do this anymore.'"

The Long Road to Recovery

Admitting to having anorexia or bulimia can be hard for anyone. But it can be particularly hard for women who are used to keeping it all together. However, acknowledging the problem and getting help is especially crucial for adults, whose bodies don't bounce back as easily as a teen's will, emphasizes Davis. Due to malnutrition, older patients are even more prone to osteoporosis, and may be at a higher risk for respiratory infections, kidney failure, heart attack, and even death.

Another hurdle women face in getting treatment is that most sufferers require inpatient therapy for weeks on end, a time-out few women can manage as easily as a teenager can. . . .

Eventually, . . . Janice and Kathy sought residential treatment, which involves weeks of one-on-one therapy in a facility to teach patients alternate ways of coping with stress. Janice, for example, learned to be more open with her husband and others about her feelings: "I used to keep everything inside. Now if something is bothering me, I'll tell them and it'll help me get my mind off things." During treatment, patients also participate in group therapy, which shows them that they're not alone. . . .

> **//** *The hardest part . . . isn't the treatment: It's how patients deal afterward.* **//**

But the hardest part, say experts, isn't the treatment: It's how patients deal afterward. Even though there is research to suggest that after eight to ten years many women with eating disorders recover, a great many people continue to suffer, according to Davis. Returning to reality can be especially tough for adults, because the demands of family and work life constantly threaten to draw them back into their unhealthy patterns. "It's a more difficult transition," says Davis. "The equilibrium in a marriage or a family has been disrupted, so you're going back to a lot of tension about what things are going to be like at home." Returning to work can be just as daunting. "They often worry about being fired or of no longer being seen as competent," says Davis.

> **❝** *Since eating disorders are strongly hereditary and are triggered by environmental factors . . . these women have good reason to worry [about their children].* **❞**

Kathy, for one, had a difficult time bridging the gap between her month-long inpatient treatment and the real world. "If I gained weight, ate something I shouldn't have eaten, or I had a day when I didn't feel like I had accomplished anything, it would set me back," Kathy recalls. Mere weeks after her discharge, she was skipping meals again. But by bolstering everything she had absorbed during her inpatient treatment with weekly therapy sessions, Kathy, who now weighs 123 pounds, has managed to keep her disorder in check.

Kathy and Janice Worry About Their Children

Even so, Kathy still faces challenges. At her daughter's soccer matches, for instance, "all the mothers bring so much food." The sight of so many treats still has the power to send Kathy into a tailspin. When she gets stressed out, she forces herself to take time out for herself: "I'll go for a walk or I'll be by myself for a little while—just enough to get my head straight and tell myself that if I'm going to be there for my family, I need to focus on what's best for me." When she returns from her walks, she always finds herself feeling better. . . .

Luckily Kathy [and] Janice . . . escaped with no long-term health problems. But their one lingering concern is the effect their ordeals might have on their children. Since eating disorders are strongly hereditary and are triggered by environmental factors—like the example set by one's own mother—these women have good reason to worry. Unfortunately, in Janice's case, the worst-case scenario has already happened: Her 15-

year-old daughter is anorexic. Shortly after Janice emerged from inpatient therapy, her five-foot-six daughter starved herself down to 100 pounds. "She was lying, hiding her food. It was a fight to get her to eat dinner," Janice says. "It felt all too familiar." Her daughter is now in recovery, following intensive treatment, and mother and daughter are concentrating on seeing each other through it. "I tell myself that there's no point in blaming myself," she says. "But it's hard."

While . . . these women may always be haunted by their disorders, they are hopeful that the worst is behind them.

7

Athletes Are More Vulnerable to Anorexia than Nonathletes

Lynette Lamb

Lynette Lamb is a freelance writer and editor of Daughters, *a magazine for parents of girls.*

Girls who are involved in athletics are at greater risk of developing anorexia than those who do not participate in organized sports. Further, sports that involve individual judging—such as gymnastics, ice skating, and diving—or endurance—such as running and swimming—cause girls to be most vulnerable to eating disorders. One of the factors contributing to the high rate of eating disorders among young female athletes is that male coaches often transfer their knowledge of male athletes to female athletes and demand that they maintain excessively low body fat percentages. Parents of girls involved in sports should be vigilant and talk to their daughters and their daughters' coaches at the first sign of an eating disorder.

Mom: "I wish you'd eat more dinner."
    Daughter: "I ate plenty. Besides, fat runners lose races."
    Mom: "You're hardly fat. And don't athletes need calories for energy?"
    Daughter: "The leaner I am, the better time I'll make. Just watch!"
    Participating in sports certainly gives your daughter exercise and confidence and teaches her about teamwork. However, athletic involvement is no panacea. No matter how active your

Lynette Lamb, "Girl Athletes and Eating Disorders," *Daughters*, vol. 7, March/April 2002, pp. 1–3. Copyright © 2002 by Dads & Daughters, Duluth, MN. $24.95/1 year. 888-849-8476. www.daughers.com. Reproduced by permission.

daughter is, no matter how seriously involved in her sport, she could still be worried about her weight and could still be dieting. And that may put her at risk for an eating disorder.

In fact, if she's an athlete in certain sports, such as gymnastics or track, she is more likely than the average girl to have an eating disorder. Eating disorders (ED) are on the rise among female athletes, says Mary Jo Kane, director of the Tucker Center for Research on Girls and Women in Sport. "An alarming number of female athletes and their coaches have bought into the notion that 'thin wins.'"

A Serious Problem

Just how significant is the problem of eating disorders among female athletes? Try this out for size: Thirteen percent of female athletes suffer from eating disorders versus just 3 percent of the general female population. That's what eating disorder specialist Dr. Craig Johnson (with Laureate Psychiatric Clinic in Tulsa, Oklahoma) and his colleagues found in a recent study of female athletes at 11 NCAA Division I schools.

And even that alarmingly high rate is what Johnson calls a conservative estimate. Despite a large sample and rigorous methodology, the study was slightly flawed because the NCAA banned follow-up calls by the researchers. All of which has left Johnson and his colleagues believing that eating disorder rates among college female athletes might be higher than their study showed.

An additional 16 percent of respondents reported a drive for thinness comparable to eating disorder patients, he says. And 19 percent of the total group reported a level of body dissatisfaction comparable to ED patients, Johnson says.

Certain Sports Are Riskier

Unsurprisingly, sports are not created equal when it comes to eating disorder risk. The highest risk sports are ones based on judging—gymnastics, ice skating, and diving—or endurance—track/cross-country and swimming.

What is it about these particular sports that puts girls at greater risk? In the judged sports, says Johnson, girls compete in scanty or tight-fitting clothing and are thus concerned about "appearance thinness." They know from experience that judges, influenced by popular culture, tend to reward thinness, independent of a girl's skill in the sport. The gymnastics community, which has seen many ED victims and at least one well-publicized death (that of U.S. gymnast Christy Henrich), has been particularly at fault, says Johnson. He adds, however, that it has begun addressing this issue lately, with gymnasts' weights going up again.

In endurance sports like running, athletes are more concerned with "performance thinness"—the belief that the lower their percentage of body fat, the better their performance will be. While that is often true for male endurance athletes, it's a dangerous idea for women and girls, Johnson says.

Women and girls need at least 17 percent body fat to menstruate, and 22 to 25 percent body fat for normal fertility. Combine dieting with a training regimen, and girl athletes often stop menstruating (a condition known as amenorrhea). Amenorrhea contributes to an obsession with food, leading to a vicious—and often deadly—cycle.

One of the scariest things about dieting, says Johnson, is that a subgroup of people seems to have a genetic liability related to weight loss. When the weight of those people drops too low, it triggers a compulsion to diet that takes on a life of its own—almost like alcoholism. "It's a chemical crapshoot," he says.

> *Eating disorders (ED) are on the rise among female athletes.*

Despite these hazards, the NCAA survey found that fully 70 percent of female athletes aspired to get their body fat lower than the dangerous 17 percent threshold. "It's male coaches trying to transfer their knowledge of male athletes and performance onto female athletes." Training girls in a method that equates low body fat with peak performance can bring disastrous results, Johnson says. "All of us need to understand the risk of weight loss and realize that girls' weight loss is not a benign behavior."

Anorexia Can Be Deadly

In fact, eating disorders are often deadly. University of Minnesota psychiatrist and eating disorder specialist Dr. Scott Crow says ED have the second highest death rates of any mental illness (only opium addicts have a higher one), and the highest suicide rates. In a 10-year study of anorexics, Crow found that 10 percent had died of their disease, either from suicide or from medical complications like heart failure.

> *Thirteen percent of female athletes suffer from eating disorders versus just 3 percent of the general female population.*

Even if a daughter recovers from an eating disorder, her bones and major organs may not. Young women with eating disorders are at a higher risk for osteoporosis, infertility, and heart problems. Recovered victims often never make up for the bone loss or heart damage they have suffered, and frequently cannot bear children.

Self-Esteem Is Important

For all these reasons, Johnson has this advice for parents: "If your girl says she wants to lose weight, you should approach that with the same seriousness that you would approach her saying that she wants to have cosmetic surgery or to use birth control pills." Treating dieting as a trivial matter has helped lead to our culture's alarming rise in eating disorders, he says.

If you suspect a problem with your athlete-daughter, speak to her about it right away with concern but without confrontation, and then talk to her coach. Parents and coaches need to work together to help girls with eating disorders, emphasizes former college track coach Vanessa Seljeskog. Although coaches are not eating disorder experts, they can be key parental and therapeutic allies, but only if they are educated about ED, she says. Meanwhile, forcing your girl out of her sport may not be a good approach unless her health is in immediate danger, Seljeskog adds.

As for how parents can help prevent ED in their daughter-athletes in the first place, improving her self-esteem seems to be key. Johnson's NCAA study showed that black female athletes, who had much lower rates of eating disorders, also scored far higher on self-esteem measures than did white female athletes.

A girl's self-esteem benefits if it is not entirely dependent on her sport. Former collegiate track star and recovered anorexic JoAnna Deeter cautions, "Running defined me totally; it was all I had."

Ten Ways Parents Can Help Prevent Anorexia

1. Maintain positive, healthy attitudes and behaviors toward your own body. Your daughter is learning from the things you say and do.

2. Avoid conveying a weightist attitude that says, in effect, "I will like you more if you lose weight." Stop reinforcing the idea that fat is "bad" and thin is "good."

3. Avoid categorizing foods into good/safe/low-fat and bad/dangerous/high-fat. Be a good role model in regard to sensible eating, exercise, and self-acceptance.

4. Don't avoid activities such as swimming simply because they call attention to your weight and shape. Don't choose or avoid certain clothes for the same reason.

5. Exercise for the joy of feeling your body move, not to purge fat from it.

6. Teach your girl to take people seriously for what they say, feel, and do, not for how slender or well put-together they appear.

7. Help her appreciate and resist the ways in which the media distort the true diversity of human body types and imply that a slender body means power, excitement, popularity, or perfection.

8. Educate your daughter about various forms of prejudice, including weightism, and help her understand her responsibility to prevent it.

9. Encourage your daughter to be active and enjoy what her body can do and feel like. Don't limit her calories unless a doctor requests you do so for a medical problem.

10. Promote her self-esteem in intellectual, athletic, and social endeavors. A well-rounded sense of self and solid self-esteem are the best antidotes to dieting and disordered eating.

8

Anorexia Is Becoming a Problem in Asia

Jessi Hempel

Jessi Hempel is a freelance writer based in Hong Kong.

Once thought to be an exclusively Western disorder that affected only white middle- and upper-class women, anorexia is now being diagnosed with increasing frequency throughout the world, especially in Asia. In Singapore and Tokyo, doctors are diagnosing eating disorders in as many as one in thirty-six people—the majority of whom are women. Some health professionals blame Asia's growing weight-loss industry for the increasing number of anorexic women. However, others maintain that the weight-loss industry is a by-product of the pervasive modernization and Westernization that is sweeping across Asia. Looking to modern, western women as guides, Asian women have begun to embrace a slimmer body type.

Shortly after Brenda, 20, did poorly on her final exams, she became obsessed with food and began to diet.

"I felt bad about myself because I'd failed," she said, refusing to share her last name out of shame. "I wanted to prove I had discipline."

So she planned out sparse meals each morning, cut out meat entirely, and began exercising for hours daily. When she'd lost 20 pounds—more than a sixth of her body weight—her mother brought her to a new clinic for eating disorders that had just opened at Hong Kong's Prince of Wales Hospital. The clinic's founder, Dr. Sing Lee, diagnosed her with an illness she

Jessi Hempel, "Eating Disorders Grow Among Hong Kong Women," www.wom ensenews.org, August 8, 2002. Copyright © 2002 by Women's eNews. Reproduced by permission.

had never heard of: anorexia nervosa.

Anorexia, a psychiatric disease in which patients starve themselves, was once thought to be a Western disease that affected white middle- and upper-class women. But the demographics of the illness are changing. Eating disorders are being diagnosed in Asian cities from Seoul to Bangkok. In Singapore and Tokyo, the numbers of patients rival the United States, where as many as one in 36 people have eating disorders, according to the National Eating Disorder Association. More than 90 percent of people with eating disorders are women and girls.

In Hong Kong, there are 25 times as many patients with eating disorders as there were 15 years ago, according to Lee. "In the late 1980s, I'd see one or two patients a year on the hospital's psychiatric ward," he said. "Now psych wards see that many in a week."

Until recently, the hospital psychiatric ward is where Hong Kong's patients received treatment once their physical complications became dangerous to their health. People with bulimia, a related eating disorder in which patients consume up to 20,000 calories in one seating, then purge the food through induced vomiting, went undiagnosed and untreated because their symptoms are easier to hide.

"These patients needed a lot of time with the doctor in counseling," Lee said. "The medical system didn't have the capacity to meet their needs."

So two years ago, Lee opened Hong Kong Eating Disorder Clinic, the city's only clinic for patients suffering from anorexia and bulimia. The clinic received 300 phone calls from potential patients during its first week in operation. With a piano, a karaoke machine, and a pile of fashion magazines, its interior looks more like a living room than a clinic in the sterile hospital that houses it. But in Hong Kong, it is the frontline in the battle to confront eating disorders.

A Booming Market for Diet Aids

Many health professionals blame the sudden increase in patients with eating disorders on Hong Kong's ballooning weight-loss industry. Consumers can purchase diarrhea-inducing herbal teas, slimming pills, cellulite creams and products to tone and thin face muscles. And fitness centers are sprouting up on nearly every city block in business districts.

"My friends skip lunch routinely and everyone is on a diet," said Eunice Leung, 24. A long-haired woman in stylish clothes that accentuate a thin frame, Leung attends university during the school year in New York. "It's OK for women to have a little tummy in America. There's more pressure in Hong Kong. Even if you're flat, you want to be even smaller."

But most doctors agree the weight-loss industry is a byproduct of a larger phenomenon in Asia: modernization.

"Asia once embraced many different types of bodies as beautiful," said Kathleen Kwok, a clinical psychologist who works with Lee at the Hong Kong Eating Disorders Clinic. "Because people were poorer, a plump body symbolized wealth and the ability to bear children."

> *Eating disorders are being diagnosed in Asian cities from Seoul to Bangkok.*

A 2000 study conducted through Chinese University compared body image perception in Shenzhen, a city along the China-Hong Kong border, a rural Chinese village in the Hunan Province and Hong Kong. Women in rural China preferred slightly larger body types on average and they dieted less despite being slightly heavier. Hong Kong women weighed less, dieted more and strove to be thinner. The study concluded that modernization equates success with "young, slender, more glamorous women."

Brenda agrees that modern pressures caused her to develop anorexia. "It wasn't my weight ultimately," she said. "I was stressed out and I needed to control something in my life." After two years of weekly 45-minute counseling sessions with Kwok, she considers herself to be recovered. She has been accepted to a university and says she no longer obsesses about food.

"I was lucky because my mother was a nurse," Brenda said. "She knew to bring me to the clinic."

Western Therapy Clashes with Asian Expectations

But other Asian families have trouble embracing the Western style of therapy used to treat eating disorders, Lee says. "The mother—or even father—often wants to know what happens in therapy or they ask the therapist to say or do something to their daughter," he said. "However, from a Western perspective, the therapist is accountable to the client, not parents, in terms of confidentiality."

Kwok said one mother called every time her daughter came in and asked how much weight the daughter had gained. "She got upset when I wouldn't tell her," Kwok said.

A greater barrier to treatment is the lack of information. Philippa Yu, 28, is a social worker at the Hong Kong Eating Disorder Association, a nonprofit formed last year to provide information and support to families of patients with eating disorders. She said many patients search for information about eating disorders on English-language Internet sites. Last year, the association began a hotline for eating disorders. In the first half of 2002, the hotline has received more calls than in all of 2001. Also, Lee recently published a Chinese-language book on eating disorders that's in its second printing.

As the problem grows, so does the need for better and more treatment. Lee's clinic has treated 350 patients. In the next few years, Lee hopes to expand his clinic in Hong Kong and to work with colleagues to set up similar clinics in Beijing, Shanghai, Guangzhou and Bangkok.

Like Brenda, many patients are recovering and leading normal lives again. But with eating disorders striking as many as 1 in 20 Hong Kong women ages 15 to 24, this clinic barely makes a dent in the need.

9

Anorexics Derive a Sense of Control from Their Behavior

Kyffin Webb

Kyffin Webb is a recovering anorexic.

Like many anorexics, I derived a sense of control over my life by controlling the amount of food and the frequency with which I ate. I used food restriction as a way of coping with the stresses of my life. I began by skipping breakfast and then all meals during my junior year of high school. By spring of that year I was diagnosed with anorexia. Despite being under a doctor's care, I continued to lose weight and was hospitalized a few months later. Although I was aware of the damage anorexia was doing to my body, I refused to give up control over the food I ate—the only control I felt I had over anything in my life. I was ultimately admitted to an eating disorder treatment center and began a healthy eating regimen and learned new skills to deal with the difficulties in my life. I still struggle with anorexia and understand that recovery will take a long time.

Whenever I felt like my life was out of control I turned to the one thing I could control: my food intake.

I started out just skipping breakfast, but I soon began skipping breakfast and lunch. Before I knew it, I was skipping all meals. I would go to school each day, and only chew gum. But even the gum I chewed counted as food, because, after all, each stick had five calories. After school I would go to work until 8 P.M.

When I finally got home in the evenings I would have a plate full of vegetables, and then go to bed. I was constantly thinking of food, and how many calories were in everything I ate, from gum to toothpaste. I allowed myself to have 300 calories a day. Needless to say, my weight began to severely drop and my health began to fade. "But," I thought, "at least I am in control."

At lunch the other kids would tease me, and try to feed me, like I didn't know how.

"C'mon Kyff. One potato chip won't kill you. My God!"

Even my teachers were commenting.

"Well, maybe if you ate you wouldn't be so cold." The Friday before Spring Break my science teacher asked me to stay after class.

In Denial

"Kyffin, are you anorexic?" she asked casually, as if she had rehearsed what she had said to me.

"No," I snapped, "I eat. I just eat healthily." I thought that would be the end of it.

I was planning to have a fun spring break. I was going to Florida with my mom and dad, and we were going to relax and enjoy the bright, southern sunrays for a week. But instead of an eight day trip, it turned into a four day trip.

> **❛❛ Whenever I felt like my life was out of control I turned to the one thing I could control: my food intake. ❜❜**

It was a beautiful spring night. The weather was perfect. We were eating dinner at an outdoor restaurant overlooking the ocean, when my mother interrupted me to say, "Kyffin, if you don't eat we are going home tomorrow!"

My father chipped in with, "If you don't eat, when we get home, I am taking your car away."

I looked down at my plate of cold and pathetic-looking chicken and started to cry. I buried my face in my napkin, and sobbed. I didn't care if the people around us saw. In frustration I blurted out, "I just can't eat! I have rules about eating, okay?!" The warm ocean breeze now felt icy and I left the table. I walked back to the hotel alone. My parents kept their promises, and the next morning we headed back home. The instant we arrived home, they took me to the doctor, and it was then that I was diagnosed with Anorexia Nervosa.

> *My weight began to severely drop and my health began to fade. 'But,' I thought, 'at least I am in control.'*

During the next month, I lost five pounds a week. My weight became so low that I had to be home schooled near the end of my junior year. My body had to eat something in order to survive, so it ate away at my muscle until I had none left. After my muscle, it ate away at whatever it could. I couldn't get up in the morning without every bone in my body aching. I felt dizzy constantly, and could barely walk up stairs. My memory began to fade, and I couldn't concentrate on anything, due to my body's constant hunger. One morning, as I was brushing my teeth, I felt exceptionally dizzy. I waited for the feeling to pass, but it never did. As I turned the corner of the hall, and walked toward the living room, everything suddenly went black. When I regained consciousness I was lying face up on the floor with my mother standing over me. When I heard her scream, "Call 911!" I knew I had fainted. Moments later an ambulance arrived at my house, and I was taken to the hospital. An I.V. was inserted into my forearm vein, and for two gruesome hours I was intravenously fed fluids.

Anorexia Worsens

I was in the hospital when my best friend Stacy gave birth to a beautiful baby girl, named MaKenzie. I spent the entire month of June in the hospital, and when I was finally released I headed straight to another hospital. This time it was to visit. I saw Stacy and MaKenzie two days after she was born. We had both been in and out of hospitals, both our bodies were going through some pretty rough stuff, and we had both lost a part of our cherished teenage freedom.

Stacy was very busy with her newborn over the summer, and we hardly saw each other. But I continued to count on Anorexia to be there with me at all times. Anorexia never told me to eat. With Anorexia's help, I showed no signs of improvement all summer long. My hair began to fall out in clumps, my skin was yellow, my nails turned brittle and cracked, and I was consistently fainting. I lost my hearing in one ear and my monthly periods. My doctor informed me that I would lose all my hair within six months, and if I didn't get my period back, I would lose the ability to have kids. She also warned me that I was at high risk for heart attack. I was slowly dying, but I didn't want to give up the only control I had.

I went to school for two days my senior year and my weight fell. I was taken out of school and placed into another hospital. After two months my weight was still the same. Something major had to be done, and the next step was taken. In the beginning of September I was taken 12 hours away, and placed in an eating disorder hospital in Pennsylvania, called Renfrew.

> *I just can't eat! I have rules about eating!*

At the hospital, my first thought was, "What is the quickest way to get out of here?" The halls smelled like pills and medicine. As I sat and waited for the head nurse to introduce herself, I carefully scanned the hallway. The carpet was an ugly rose color. The white walls were covered with artwork, that said things like, "Love yourself now", "Everyone is unique", and "Celebrate your differences."

What a joke, I thought. As I sat and waited, other girls came up to me smiling and introducing themselves. They all looked genuinely happy, something I hadn't felt in a long time. I wondered how everyone could seem so worry-free in a hospital!

Hospitalization Helps

I spent my first three days at Renfrew crying. I missed my home, my friends, and my old eating ways. But, unlike at home, I received an enormous amount of support from girls who were going through the exact same thing as me. I could finally relate to someone! I began to feel better. I spent the next month in a large house with 40 other women and girls who all shared eating disorders.

Mealtimes were the most difficult times, and there were five meals a day. We all sat in a small dining room and were served our meals. We had counselors watching over our shoulders for the entire meal. We were expected to eat every last drop on our plate. If we left one carrot stick or half of an olive laying on our plate, we were punished in the worst way an Anorexic can think of. We were forced to drink a tall, thick glass of Ensure, a weight-gain drink.

Every day I would wake up at 5:45 A.M. and change into a thin plastic gown. I would head to the nurse's station to be weighed and have my vital signs taken, along with all the other girls. The line was always long, and I'd have to stand in the cold, dark hallway for at least 30 minutes. Once I was weighed and examined I would return to my room and try to fall back to sleep. Yet my dreaded alarm never failed to go off once again at 7:30 A.M. and all 40 of us would then head to the dining room for breakfast. After breakfast we met in groups with names like Coping Skills, Yoga, Expression Art, or Recognizing and Handling Feelings. There I started to learn about new ways to cope with the tough stuff in my life, rather than restricting food.

After group we would return to the dining room for lunch. Then I had more groups until snack time, which was at 3 P.M. After a snack I had free time/visiting time for an hour and a half. Since my parents were 12 hours away and could never visit, I would usually sleep. It was a very depressing time of my day. After my catnap I would head once again to the dining room for supper. After supper I had therapy. Then I would end my day with another snack in the dining hall at 9 P.M. Lights went out at 10 P.M. each night. The days were long, slow and difficult. I missed my home more and more with each passing day. One day, halfway through my stay at Renfrew, the doctor called me into her office. I thought she wanted to check in with me and make sure everything was alright.

Seventy-Year-Old Bones

"Come on in, Kyffin. Have a seat. I am afraid I have some bad news," Dorris warned as she filed through my records. I sat in the overstuffed chair wondering what was wrong. My first thoughts were that something had happened to my parents. It never occurred to me, the bad news had to do with me. She explained to me that I had osteoporosis. "You have the bones of a 70 year old," she told me. "This means absolutely no more caffeine, no playing contact sports, and no more forgetting to take your calcium supplements. Ever. For the rest of your life. Are you listening to me?" I was listening alright, and so was my mom when she was phoned minutes later. This was the worst news yet.

> **❝❝ I was slowly dying, but I didn't want to give up the only control I had. ❞❞**

In early October, I was released from Renfrew, and returned home to Kentucky. The first weeks back at home were hard. My grandmother was dying, and since I had been away so long, I really didn't have a social life. My life consisted of numerous doctor visits, which I dreaded terribly. It seemed every doctor wanted to know my weight. That was, and still is, a very sensitive subject for me. I was on my own now. My parents were instructed to let me be in charge of my own recovery. This meant I had to feed myself, and plan my meals by myself. There was no one looking over my shoulder, no one to make sure I was getting enough calories. My weight stopped rising, as my grandmother's health started failing. I started to restrict again, and lost the weight I had gained once out of the hospital. I fell to five pounds less than what I had weighed when I was discharged from Renfrew.

Slow Recovery

I wish I could tell you that I have totally recovered since then, but the truth is that I'm only at the very beginning of a long road to recovery. I am still struggling to stabilize and get my weight up to, at least, what it was when I left Renfrew. I still count every calorie I eat, hide from all mirrors, and refuse to be weighed unless it is absolutely necessary. Every day I struggle to eat enough just to maintain my weight. I feel fat after eating anything, whether it be an apple or a salad.

As I fight to take life back into my own hands, I realize I am going to have to do something very scary. I'm going to have to let go of my best friend, Anorexia. She can never be a part of my life and I won't be able to rely on her for help again, but I know I'm going to be okay. Anorexia was never very good at being a best friend, anyway.

10

Anorexics Lose Control Due to Their Behavior

Lana D'Amico

Lana D'Amico is a former intern at Dance Magazine *and an associate editor at Sterling Macfadden Partnership, publisher of sports, music, and entertainment magazines. She is also a freelance writer for several women's magazines.*

In order to improve my ballet performance and achieve the "ballerina look," I decided I needed to be thinner. I began skipping meals and losing weight. Although my ballet instructor and my parents voiced their concerns, I insisted that restricting my food intake was not hurting me and would help my dancing. After a summer of eating only one meal a day and dancing strenuously, I was showing the physical symptoms of anorexia. Unlike many young women with eating disorders, I did not need professional help to realize that I had lost control of my eating behavior. With my family's help, I was able to slowly begin eating again.

I'm not sure when it started. What I do know is that it wasn't about being thin enough for a guy, or about not being happy in my life, and it certainly wasn't because I thought I was fat. For "real" life, I knew that I was fine. But for ballet, I wasn't quite thin enough, or so I believed.

I'd wanted to be a ballerina for as long as I could remember. While most teens were at the mall, dating, or getting that perfect prom dress, I was at ballet. Ballet class wasn't just something I went to for fun; it was my whole life. When I wasn't at dance, I was watching videos of my favorites, listening to clas-

Lana D'Amico, "Not Thin Enough: When Losing Weight Becomes Losing Control," originally published as "When What You Weigh Becomes Who You Are," from *Co-ed Confessions*. Reproduced by permission of Dorchester Media.

sical music and envisioning choreography, or daydreaming about being onstage.

To this day, I have a hard time saying that I was anorexic. I certainly wasn't bulimic. But while I may not have starved myself completely or binged and purged, I definitely had some serious issues about food. I suppose that anorexia is the closest description to what I put myself through.

> ***// For ballet, I wasn't quite thin enough, or so I believed. //***

I hear stories about girls whose teachers demand that they get thin, but my ballet teacher, Frank Ohman—a wonderfully talented man who had been a soloist in the New York City Ballet—did not encourage me to lose weight. He actually called my mother once, to ask if I was unwell. "She looked fine before," he told her. "Lana's getting too thin now—and it's happened really fast. I'm concerned." I can't ever recall Mr. Ohman putting anyone down because of their weight. Like a true professional, he was more concerned with ability, potential, and one's level of desire to be there.

Even though my mom got annoyed at me and may have been a little embarrassed about the call, I didn't think too much about it.

Only One Meal a Day

Then, when I was about 17, and deeply focused on a professional career, my once-curvy figure became a thing of the past. My legs were like those of most dancers: a mass of muscles. But the rest of me was skin and bones. My ribcage was completely visible from front to back. My arms looked as though they'd snap, and my face looked way too large for the rest of me.

In 1995, I got accepted to the Richmond Ballet's summer dance program. Faced with competing against talented dancers from all across the country, I was mentally and physically pushed to the limit. I worked hard in Virginia, and cut my intake of food down to one meal a day. I would dance from ten in the morning until six at night; eating only once—sounds insane, right?

That summer, I stopped getting my period. Instead of becoming alarmed, though, I knew it meant I was losing weight. I'd arrived in Virginia at 5'4" and 110 pounds. By the time I left, I weighed a mere 98 pounds.

> **//** *I knew something was wrong. For the first time, I looked in the mirror and saw what I really looked like.* **//**

Although I'd learned a lot in my time away, I was eager to come home, see my friends and family, and rest. I can still recall what went through my mind as I took my bow in our final workshop performance—I don't want to dance; I'm tired.

I thought my dancing was stronger, but overall, I was exhausted. When my parents came to get me, they were worried. Through happy tears at seeing me for the first time in a few months, my mom said, "You look terrible."

Slow Recovery

At this point, I knew something was wrong. For the first time, I looked in the mirror and saw what I really looked like. Back at home, my friends said, "What happened to you? Did you not eat a bite the whole summer?"

Not exactly flattering. I wanted to shout, "But you should see how much better I've gotten!"

I knew I had to eat normally and snap out of it. I was tired of hurting my parents and myself. My mother talked of taking me to see a therapist if I didn't get back in a normal eating pattern, I panicked—I didn't want that! So, very slowly, I began to eat a little more, to respond better to my hunger rather than suppressing it. Because I always ate dinner with my parents, they didn't know how little I was eating at other times. I'd be voracious at dinner with them, therefore presenting a seemingly healthy appetite.

Once I started eating properly again—wouldn't you know it? My dancing got better! With more energy, I was better able to attack steps and not be completely beat after classes and rehearsals. When I began to menstruate again, I knew that I was finally back on track. Three months without a menstrual period can be hazardous to one's health, especially for a growing girl.

When I think back, I realize what the problem stemmed from. There's a lot of pressure on young girls. We feel that we need to look a certain way to fit a particular mold. For me, that mold was what I perceived as "the ballerina look." For others, it's something else. Let me say that many ballerinas do not look anorexic. Sure, there are some—but it's nearly impossible to maintain such a low body weight and still have the stamina that ballet demands.

Regaining Control

Instead of shedding a pound or two, I lost control and lost sight of what I really looked like. I was obsessed with being reed-thin, and didn't realize that I'd be too tired to achieve my original goal. It doesn't matter how skinny you look in your costume if you're too tired to dance with the necessary bravura. I consider myself lucky, though. I was able to gain control of my eating before it became even more of a problem for me.

Sometimes I remind myself of what happened. With the pressures of a professional ballet career behind me now, I have to say I feel better in my skin. Oh, I still daydream about what could have been, and I wouldn't take back one minute of practice for anything in the world. I've continued dancing for the pure love of it, and I still adore going to the ballet.

The regimen of dance taught me about concentration, passion, goals, dedication, and plain old hard work. My ballet mentor and I are still good friends, and when I pop into his class he's happy to see that I look healthy. And when my parents get on my case about something, I listen.

11
Poor Body Image Leads to Anorexia

Kathiann M. Kowalski

Kathiann M. Kowalski is a former environmental lawyer who now writes frequently for many youth and teen magazines.

Movie stars and fashion models—obsessed with thinness and often anorexic—become role models for teens with poor body image. Young girls trying to meet the unrealistic standards of beauty and thinness set by the media may become anorexic as well. Instead of encouraging teens to accept healthy bodies of all sizes, the images young people see on television, in the movies, and in magazines pressure them to be thin at any cost.

Brianna slipped quietly out of the house before dawn. She had lost 30 pounds by dieting, but now the weight was creeping back. She decided to try non-stop exercising for three days. Brianna wasn't thinking about missing school or even being alone by herself on the street. She would start walking and just keep going.

Fifteen hours later, Brianna walked into a police station. Her feet ached, and her sweat-pants were covered with burrs from wandering through a park. She was exhausted, scared, and hungry.

A poor body image had led to Brianna's eating disorder and depression. Her grand exercise plan failed, but it had one good outcome. Brianna finally got help dealing with her problem.

Body image is the way you see your body and how you feel about it. People with a healthy body image view themselves re-

Kathiann M. Kowalski, "Body Image: How Do You See Yourself?" *Current Health 2*, vol. 29, March 2003, pp. 6–11. Copyright © 2003 by the Weekly Reader Corporation. Reproduced by permission.

alistically and like their physical selves. People with a poor body image feel dissatisfied with their bodies, regardless of whether they are objectively healthy.

Different factors influence a teen's body image. "Certainly the media are setting standards for how girls and boys should look, defining what is beautiful in our culture," says Mimi Nichter. When the University of Arizona professor interviewed girls for her book, *Fat Talk: What Girls and Their Parents Say About Dieting*, most girls chose a "Barbie-doll" look: tall, thin, and large-breasted.

> **❝ The media are setting standards for how girls and boys should look, defining what is beautiful in our culture. ❞**

That same image pervades many ads on television and in magazines. When it comes to males, the media emphasize a tall, lean, muscular look. "People are paid to create an image or an illusion," says Sarah Stinson, head of the eating disorders program at Fairview Red Wing Health Services in Minnesota.

Only about 2 percent of women are as thin as most models, says the National Eating Disorders Association. Models work full-time with exercise trainers, makeup artists, and others to maintain their appearance. At photo shoots, clips and weights mold clothes to flatter a model's body. Once images are shot, computer artists take over. They airbrush pictures to remove any flaws. They can even change the shape of the bodies in the pictures. Thus, the standard media images of beauty often aren't true to life.

Faced with such unrealistic ideals, most teens feel worse about their bodies after reading teen fashion magazines. For those who felt unaccepted or unappreciated in their social environment—up to one-third of girls in one study—the effects lasted longer, according to Eric Stice at the University of Texas at Austin.

"From my perspective," says Stice, "this study is very damning for the mass media." In real life, he adds, most boys think a starved waif look is ugly for girls. And most girls don't like seeing mega-muscles on guys.

Peer pressure also influences a teen's body image. "Teasing

can be very painful," says Nichter. "Kids seem to remember that for a very long time."

Frequent talking about weight can wear down someone's body image too. "I guess I started thinking I was fat at the start of high school," says Brianna. "Girls talk about it all the time at school—who's on diets. I would compare myself to other people, and I guess I thought I was fat."

"The majority of young women feel insecure," says Stinson. "What's happening is they're projecting those insecurities on each other, and you're getting this very competitive environment."

Families factor in too. When Brianna was little, her father sometimes commented on her eating a lot. Her brother sometimes called her a "fat pig." In other families, parents may tell a boy to eat so he grows up "big and strong." Or they may wistfully say that a daughter has "such a pretty face"—implying that the rest of her body is ugly.

Internalizing Negative Messages

Young people internalize those messages. In a study by the Centers for Disease Control and Prevention (CDC), around 30 percent of students thought they were overweight. In reality, less than 14 percent of students were "at risk for becoming overweight." (The term refers to students whose body mass index was above the 85th percentile.)

> *The standard media images of beauty often aren't true to life.*

Yet the 14 percent figure is also a problem. Nearly one-third of students get little or no physical activity, reports the CDC. Higher weight and a sedentary lifestyle increase the risks for diabetes, heart disease, and other health problems. Meanwhile, young people at the higher ranges of the weight scale often feel more frustrated by the gap between what they see in the mirror and what they see in the media.

Puberty complicates things. Girls get taller and gain an average of 25 pounds. They need the added fat for breast development and to enable them to conceive and carry babies as adults.

"Young women don't believe that they should gain fat," says Stinson. "They're terrified of it and don't understand the healthy role of natural body fat in development."

Boys get taller and more muscular as their bodies mature. That's generally consistent with our culture's ideal for males. But not all boys mature at the same rate. And not everyone gains muscle like the images featured in sports and fitness magazines.

When teens have a poor body image, self-esteem dips. Relationships suffer too. Conversations with friends may center on dieting and exercise, to the exclusion of other topics. Teens focus more on how they look than on what they want to accomplish in life. Instead of bonding with each other, teens often become competitive. That fuels feelings of isolation.

In the worst cases, eating disorders and other unhealthy behaviors develop. Eating disorders are more common among females than males. Yet the National Eating Disorders Association says about 10 percent of patients are male. (Besides a poor body image, other factors are often to blame. These include feelings of being out of control and, in some cases, a history of physical or sexual abuse.)

The Effects of Anorexia

Brianna had anorexia nervosa. She did not eat enough to maintain a normal weight for her height. Besides looking very thin, she felt weak and had dizzy spells. Because girls need a certain level of body fat to menstruate, she stopped getting her period regularly. With her immune system weakened, Brianna came down with pneumonia during her sophomore year. Plus, Brianna recalls, "I lost hair. And I was cold all the time."

In addition to these problems, anorexia can cause loss of bone density, dehydration, and downy hair on the skin. When the heart muscle weakens and blood pressure drops too low, fatal heart failure can happen. By experimenting with diet pills, Brianna added to that risk. Even "natural" weight loss products can over-stimulate the heart and cause heart attacks.

Binge eating disorder involves frequent episodes of uncontrolled eating, without regard to physical hunger or fullness. Patients suffer from guilt, shame, or disgust with their behavior. They often gain weight, which adds to any body image problems.

A person with bulimia experiences cycles of binging and purging. Even if a patient's weight stays normal, frequent vomiting causes decaying tooth enamel, swollen glands, a sore throat, and a puffy face. If patients take laxatives, they risk damage to their digestive systems and suffer from nutrient deficiencies.

Exercise bulimia compensates for eating with excessive physical activity. In her junior year of high school, actress Jamie Lynn Sigler exercised every day for hours. Her weight dropped to 90 pounds.

> **❝** *Faced with such unrealistic ideals, most teens feel worse about their bodies after reading teen fashion magazines.* **❞**

"As time went on, it began to take over my life and interfere with other things that were important to me," Jamie recalled, "like hanging out with my friends, my family, dance and theatre, and even my health." When she began thinking about suicide, Jamie finally confided in her parents. The book *Wise Girl: What I've Learned About Life, Love, and Loss* tells the story of her recovery.

Body dysmorphia, a distorted body image, can also lead to excessive bodybuilding, especially among boys. Some also abuse steroids—drugs that unnaturally mimic the hormone testosterone to spur muscle growth. Risks of steroid abuse include possible outbreaks of violence during use and depression after cycling off the drugs, plus other physical and psychological consequences.

"When you have an eating disorder, you really don't want to talk about it," said Sigler. "You get very defensive. You isolate yourself a lot." If you're concerned about a friend, keep telling that person, "I'm here for you when you're ready to talk about it."

Building a Healthier Body Image

A doctor specializing in eating disorders gave Brianna a thorough check-up and prescribed medicine to help her clinical depression. Brianna also meets regularly with a psychologist, who has given her strategies to build a healthier body image.

"She had me write a list of things I like about myself," says Brianna. "When I start comparing myself to people, I think of one of those things rather than thinking, 'Oh, she looks so good and I look so bad.'" Among other things, Brianna is very intelligent. She is a hard worker. She is great at ballet. She plays the flute beautifully. And she likes her pretty blonde hair and blue eyes.

Dance class can still be a challenge, since the other advanced students are very thin. Brianna is learning to accept that people have different body shapes: ectomorphic, mesomorphic, and endomorphic. Ectomorphic people are very thin. Mesomorphic people are muscular. Endomorphic people tend to carry more fat. Many people's bodies mix these characteristics. Thus, one part of the body may be muscular, while another part may gain fat easily.

// Thirty percent of students thought they were overweight. In reality, less than 14 percent . . . were 'at risk for becoming overweight.' //

Brianna also met with a dietitian. When she was constantly dieting, she skipped meals. By nighttime she was so hungry that she might eat half a box of cereal. Now she's eating regular meals and including a reasonable amount of fat. She feels healthier and stronger. Now that she's eating regular meals again, she socializes more with other students at lunchtime too.

Another helpful strategy is to change the pattern of "fat talk" among friends. Sometimes teens join in the talk as a way to fit in. Other times, "I feel fat" can be code for other feelings that young people feel uncomfortable talking about: loneliness, disappointment, anger, insecurity, and so on. If teens encourage each other to talk about what's really bothering them, they can break the cycle of putting their bodies down. Clearer communication also frees teens to help each other deal with problems constructively.

Unrealistic Standards of Beauty

The media emphasize unrealistic standards of beauty. But, says Stinson, "You don't have to buy into these messages." She encourages young people to become activists: Write letters to companies praising ads that show normal teens with different body shapes and sizes. Conversely, send complaints and boycott companies that exploit young people by sexualizing them or glorifying thinness.

Don't fall prey to the dieting industry either.

Even "natural" weight-loss pills can contain stimulants that cause serious health problems. And despite "money-back guarantees," diet gizmos and gimmicks don't work. If any one did work, would Americans continue to spend $40 billion a year on books, diet programs, pills, gadgets, and everything else the dieting industry produces?

You can help educate other young people about having a healthy body image. In Minnesota, teen members of Red Wing GO GIRLS! make frequent presentations to help other young people develop a positive body image. By teaching others, the teens have become role models who are very proud of their own bodies.

Self-Acceptance Is Key

"It's not your weight that determines your health," says Stinson. "It's your lifestyle." Here are some tips for a healthy lifestyle:

• Eat a variety of foods when you're physically hungry. Refer to the U.S. Department of Agriculture's Food Guide Pyramid (www.nal.usda.gov).

• Don't forget the calcium: The Food and Drug Administration (FDA) recommends four servings of calcium-rich foods a day for teens.

• Enjoy regular physical activities. Aim for at least 30 minutes a day most days of the week. Set realistic goals for yourself, and have a good time. The more your body can do, the better you'll feel about it.

Brianna is enjoying dance more now. She also has joined her school's swim team and enjoys the camaraderie with her teammates. When the team members feel tired after a practice, it's a good feeling. "As long as you're healthy and active, and your body is doing everything it's supposed to do, there's nothing wrong with your body shape," she says.

Based on her experience, Brianna adds this message to teens: "You're OK the way you are. Think of the many great things you are—you're like no one else. Just don't ever try to compare yourself with anyone because it's not worth it. You have to be yourself."

12

Anorexia May Have a Biological Basis

Emily Sohn

Science writer Emily Sohn has written for U.S. News & World Report, New Scientist, *and* Science.

Studies of twins provide evidence for a biological basis for eating disorders such as anorexia. Researchers have found that if one identical twin suffers from anorexia, the other twin is much more likely to develop an eating disorder. Studies also find that eating disorders tend to run in families. Scientists have discovered the location of several genes in the human genome that seem to increase the risk of anorexia. Other researchers contend that anorexia can be traced to personality traits that are hardwired into the brain. For example, anorexics are often perfectionists. Acknowledging that eating disorders are real medical illnesses may help those struggling with eating disorders and their families.

Dinnertime was always stressful at the Corbett house. Every evening at 6 o'clock precisely, the five kids would take their assigned places at the table between Mom and Dad. Food was served family style, and whatever you took, you had to eat. You couldn't have dessert until after you had finished everything on your plate. "It was not a relaxing time to sit at the table and eat," recalls Cathie Reinard, 35, about her childhood in Rochester, N.Y. But the rigid rules just added to an underlying tension. As the kids got older, it became clear that most meals would end with Mom's excusing herself, going into the bathroom, and making herself throw up.

Messages about food were inconsistent and confusing to the Corbett kids, especially the three girls. On the one hand, dessert was served every night, and food was always part of family gatherings. On the other hand, the girls, all petite and athletic, were constantly being told they were fat—both by Mom at home and by their gymnastics coach, who wanted his athletes lean. Food was forbidden fruit. Between-meal snacks were prohibited, and the padlock on the kitchen pantry kept little hands away from the candy, Pop-Tarts, and soda stashed inside.

With so many rules and restrictions, it's no wonder that all three girls developed eating disorders, say the Corbetts, now grown and with families of their own. Cathie started sticking her fingers down her throat in high school, after a gymnastics injury prevented her from working out. Her identical twin, Bonnie, developed anorexia in college, dropping 50 pounds off her 5-foot, 120-pound frame in six months. It began, she says, when a boyfriend pointed out her growing beer belly. Their older sister, Liz, 38, was an "exercise bulimic": To make up for eating sprees, she repeatedly pushed her body to the point of injury from daily workouts that could last for three hours or more. Even their brother Daryl, 41, lost his appetite for a few months when he broke up with his first girlfriend in college.

Their mother, Margery Bailey, still feels very guilty about her children's problems. And no wonder. When Bonnie was hospitalized with anorexia at age 19 in 1985, Bailey says the doctors severely restricted her visits. "I was told it was my fault."

Dysfunctional families are still a common target of blame, as is a dysfunctional culture obsessed with thinness. But as doctors learn more about eating disorders, it is becoming clear that genetics and biology may be equally important causal factors for the estimated 5 million to 10 million Americans who struggle with anorexia, bulimia, and binge-eating disorders. Although family and culture may provide the ultimate trigger, it seems increasingly likely that hormones and brain chemicals prime a certain group of people to push themselves to starvation.

A Deadly Disorder

Eating disorders are the deadliest of all psychiatric disorders, killing or contributing to the deaths of thousands every year. An estimated 50,000 people currently suffering from an eating disorder will eventually die as a result of it. Anorexics, who pursue thinness so relentlessly through diet and exercise that they drop to below 85 percent of ideal body weight, often suffer heart attacks, arthritis, osteoporosis, and other health problems. Bulimics eat uncontrollably, then compensate by throwing up, taking laxatives, or exercising obsessively—behaviors that can upset the body's chemical balance enough that it stops working.

As with depression and other serious psychiatric illnesses, eating disorders now appear to be a familial curse. Relatives of eating disorder patients are 7 to 12 times as likely to develop an eating disorder as is the general population, studies show. Depression, anxiety disorders, and other related illnesses also appear more frequently in the same families. That doesn't rule out a shared environment as a contributing factor, says psychologist Michael Strober of the University of California–Los Angeles. But, he adds, "anytime you see a disorder that runs in families, you begin to suspect some hereditary influence."

> *// Eating disorders are the deadliest of all psychiatric disorders. //*

The women in Bailey's family have been fighting a losing battle with food for generations. When Bailey was 18, her 55-pound mother starved herself to death, sneaking laxatives in the hospital until the very end. Other relatives have also suffered from anorexia. "I was always told I was fat and ugly and dumb," recalls Bailey, a 63-year-old retired nurse. She vividly remembers how she and her brothers secreted cans of food because they weren't getting enough to eat at meals. But, she concedes now, the sheer number of eating disorders in her family suggests something deeper going on.

Evidence for Biological Causes

Deadly eating disorders exist in cultures far removed from Hollywood and Madison Avenue and have been around far longer than glossy women's magazines. But if that weren't evidence enough for an underlying biology, the patients themselves are the first to say their eating disorders have a power far greater than peer pressure. Indeed, Stephanie Rose's illness had such a strong "personality" that she named it "Ed." It started with a diet to lose 8 pounds of weight gain after her freshman year of college. But her success became an obsession that landed her in the hospital nine times over the next four years. She crashed a car and a bicycle, both times after passing out from nutrient deprivation. She chugged bottles of poison-control syrup to make herself throw up, even if she had eaten only a bite of a tuna fish sandwich or a few grains of cereal. Even in the hospital, she shoved batteries in her underwear to fool the nurses when they weighed her. Talking and reading took too much energy, so she stared at the TV instead, gray-skinned, too weak to think.

At her sickest, the 5-foot, 5-inch Needham, Mass., resident weighed 75 pounds. She had a mild heart attack at age 21 as a result of her starved state. Doctors told her bluntly that she was going to die, and nurses sat with her 24 hours a day to make sure she didn't pull out her feeding tube. Now 29, fully recovered and happily married with a 15-month-old baby of her own, Rose can't believe she would flirt with death for arms that looked like toothpicks. "It was like someone took over my body," she says, "this guy, Ed."

> *Deadly eating disorders exist in cultures far removed from Hollywood and Madison Avenue.*

The most convincing evidence for genetics comes from twins. If one twin has an eating disorder, the other is far more likely to have a similar illness if the twins are identical rather than fraternal. Since identical twins are genetic clones of each other, that is powerful evidence that genes play an important role, says psychiatrist Cynthia Bulik of Virginia Commonwealth University: "Until now, people would have said there wasn't a genetic effect in anorexia. And what we're saying is that there really is, and it's not minimal."

Several groups of researchers are now hunting for the specific genes involved in eating disorders, with some promising leads. The first two comprehensive scans of the human genome have recently turned up hot spots for anorexia-linked genes on several chromosomes, including Chromosome 1, which seems to harbor genes for the most severe form of anorexia. "We now know the location of several genes in the human genome which increase risk for anorexia nervosa," says

University of Pennsylvania psychiatrist Wade Berrettini, a senior author of a study in the March 2002 issue of the *American Journal of Human Genetics*. "Prior to this, we did not." Other preliminary work is pointing to different areas of the genome that may be involved in bulimia, says psychiatrist Walter Kaye of the University of Pittsburgh.

> *Comprehensive scans of the human genome have recently turned up hot spots for anorexia-linked genes on several chromosomes.*

None of the scientists exploring the genome expects to find easy answers or simple genetic switches. Indeed, hundreds of genes are already known to influence appetite and eating regulation in some way, a testament to how complex the eating impulse really is in the grand scheme of human biology.

But some patterns are emerging. The most obvious is that 90 percent of eating disorders occur in girls and women, most often beginning in adolescence. This clue has some experts exploring the genes that control hormone production. During the teen years in most girls, estrogen-producing genes kick in, triggering puberty. And there is evidence, says Michigan State psychologist Kelly Klump, suggesting that those genes may also contribute to eating disorders in some girls: Genes appear to be involved in 17-year-old twins with eating disorders but not in 11-year-old twins, who are mostly prepubescent. But even more striking, Klump says, a study of 11-year-old twins who had gone through puberty and exhibited warning signs of the illness showed the same genetic pattern as the 17-year-olds. Klump notes, by analogy, that depression hits girls twice as hard after puberty as before.

Personality Traits

Other researchers are linking eating disorders to personality traits that are hard-wired into the brain. Anorexics tend to be Type A—anxious, perfectionist, rigid. Those traits can translate into an unhealthy body image: When a driven perfectionist sets her mind on being slender, self-control can become a measure of success. Anorexics also tend to be ritualistic about the food they eat, cutting it into tiny pieces or eating only a specific type of food at only a specific time of day.

Such an obsessive temperament often appears to be inborn. In Kathryn Carvette DeVito's case, the first signs appeared at age 7. She started having panic attacks on the school playground and became preoccupied with getting her homework perfect, starting over and over again if necessary. Then she developed some classic symptoms of obsessive-compulsive disorder: "If I touched a doorknob 15 times, everything would be OK," she says. Kathryn hit puberty earlier than her classmates, and when a doctor told her she was heavier than the average sixth grader, her obsessions turned to food. She dropped to a low of 85 pounds before seeking help when she was 19. Even now, though the 5-foot, 2-inch Boston University senior sees a psychologist weekly and has stabilized her weight at about 100 pounds, she says that she sometimes eats as little as 100 calories a day. She works out every day and does sit-ups in her bed at night.

Brain chemicals may contribute to illnesses such as Kathryn's, says the University of Pittsburgh's Kaye. It may be that people who go on to develop the anxiety and obsessiveness associated with eating disorders have abnormally high levels of serotonin, one of the brain's major chemical messengers for mood, sexual desire, and food intake. Losing weight lowers serotonin, so anorexics may stop eating in a subconscious attempt to lower their uncomfortably high serotonin levels, says psychiatrist Evelyn Attia of the New York State Psychiatric Institute. But when a person stops eating, her brain churns out even more serotonin, Attia says. So, the anorexic gets caught "in a vicious cycle where the behavior tries to compensate for the uncomfortable feeling of biochemical imbalance but can never catch up."

> *Anorexics tend to be Type A—anxious, perfectionist, rigid.*

Kaye also has evidence that the brains of recovered bulimics process serotonin in a way that is different from the brains of healthy people. It's not entirely clear yet if their brains were different before they developed the disease or if dieting caused the changes. Still, such chemical differences suggest that drugs like

Prozac, used to treat depression and compulsive behaviors, might be helpful for treating eating disorders as well. In a small study, Kaye found that Prozac, which helps the brain's pathways work better, helped prevent relapses in recovered anorexics.

A Long Road to Recovery

Despite all these biomedical advances in understanding eating disorders, victims still face a long and uncertain road to recovery. Only about half of anorexics and bulimics ever recover enough to maintain a healthy weight and positive self-image. Thirty percent of anorexics have residual symptoms that persist long into adulthood, and 1 in 10 cases remains chronic and unremitting. Without treatment, up to 20 percent of cases end in premature death.

> *Brain chemicals may contribute to [anorexia].*

Denial and resistance to treatment are fierce psychological obstacles once an eating disorder has taken hold, so scientists are looking more and more to prevention. And ironically, given the move away from cultural explanations for the disorders, the best interventions for now may still be psychosocial. Surveys show that 42 percent of children in first through third grade want to be thinner and that 81 percent of 10-year-olds are afraid of being fat. Those attitudes are clearly not genetic, and they are so pervasive that they could be pushing the genetically vulnerable over the edge. "If people never diet," Bulik says, "they might never enter into the higher-risk category for developing eating disorders."

One of the most striking examples of culture's influence comes from Fiji, where a bulky body has always been a beautiful body. Women on the South Pacific island have traditionally complimented one another for gaining weight. Food is starchy, calorie-dense, and plentiful. But when TV came to the island in 1995—with shows like *Melrose Place* and commercials celebrating thinness—the depictions of beauty radically altered Fijians' self-image—especially the girls'. According to a study published in June 2002 by Harvard psychiatrist and anthropologist Anne

Becker, by 1998 the proportion of girls at risk for developing eating disorders more than doubled to 29 percent of the population. The percentage of girls who vomited to lose weight jumped from zero to 11 percent. "We actually talked to girls who explicitly said, 'I want to be thin because I watch TV, and everyone on TV has all those things, and they're thin,'" Becker says. Likewise, non-Western immigrants to the United States are more likely to develop eating disorders than are their relatives in the homeland.

A Costly Disorder

While scientists debate and explore the causes of eating disorders, victims and their families are being hard hit financially. Hospitalization and around-the-clock care to revive a starving patient can cost more than $1,000 a day. Full recovery can take years of therapy, often involving the whole family. But because eating disorders are classified as a mental illness, insurance plans rarely cover the full costs of treatment. Kitty Westin slammed into just that painful wall. Her daughter Anna had struggled with anorexia as a teenager but seemed healthy when she came home to Chaska, Minn., after her sophomore year at the University of Oregon in Eugene. Within months, depression and anxiety again consumed Anna. She couldn't sleep. She withdrew from her family and friends. She stopped eating and spent hours at the gym every day. By summer's end, Anna, who had always been petite, could barely stand without feeling dizzy. At 5 feet, 4 inches, she weighed 82 pounds, and her vital signs were dangerously low. No matter how hard she fought the anorexia, she felt powerless. "It won't leave me alone," she told her mother.

> *" Denial and resistance to treatment are fierce psychological obstacles once an eating disorder has taken hold. "*

For the next six months, Anna checked in and out of the hospital. She would improve as an inpatient. But as soon as she went home, she'd get sick again, says Kitty Westin, who quit her job as a psychologist to take care of her daughter. The family's health insurance company, Blue Cross and Blue Shield of

Minnesota, refused to fully cover the costs of residential treatment, leaving the family to pay for whatever they could. On Feb. 17, 2000, worn out from her struggle, Anna killed herself. She was 21. Her mother, now a full-time advocate for better insurance coverage, says the family's battles with the insurance company exacerbated Anna's illness. "See, I'm not sick," Anna would say. "The insurance company says I'm not sick."

Real Illnesses

Such attitudes are slowly changing. In June 2001 the state of Minnesota settled a lawsuit against Blue Cross for repeatedly denying coverage to children with mental health problems. The settlement required the company to pay the state $8.2 million for treating families that had been refused coverage. The company is also becoming more accountable to eating disorder patients via an appointed, independent three-member panel that must review mental health appeals soon after receiving them. Westin is convinced that such a process would have saved Anna's life. "There is no doubt in my mind," she says, "that a panel would have reversed the [insurance company's] decision."

A legal acknowledgment that eating disorders are real medical illnesses brings hope to families who already know that their problems won't just go away. The grown Corbett women, for example, all still struggle with body image and health problems related to their eating disorders. Their mother, Margery, was hospitalized recently for dehydration from drinking too much alcohol and not eating enough. Liz sometimes freezes at the thought of going out to parties because she can't figure out what to wear. Cathie, who has a 3-year-old daughter and a 9-month-old son, purged during her second pregnancy and has damaged the enamel surface of her teeth from years of bulimia. Meanwhile, Bonnie continues to struggle with anorexia, 17 years after it began. She takes vitamins and mineral supplements to avoid anemia. She takes birth control pills to keep her hormone levels up. And she has recently started taking medicine to treat end-stage osteoporosis. At 35, she has the bones of an 86-year-old woman and says her hips would probably shatter if she fell. The whole family takes things one day at a time. "You get the cards you're dealt," says younger brother Rick, 31, the only sibling spared by the illness. Instead of cancer or heart disease, he says, his family got eating disorders. "Everyone has their own battles to fight," Bonnie adds. "This is ours."

13

Anorexics Often Resist Treatment

Joel Yeager

Joel Yeager is the editor in chief of Eating Disorders Today, *a newsletter for those recovering from eating disorders and for their families.*

People with anorexia often refuse treatment. Some deny that they have a problem; others are aware of their disorder but are too ashamed to seek help. In certain cases, particularly when dealing with adolescents, doctors might have to to treat a patient even when he or she actively resists. There are psychological as well as legal consequences to treating a patient against his or her will, however, thus most physicians prefer to convince the patient to accept treatment voluntarily. Nevertheless, if a patient's life is in immediate danger, treatment must proceed with or without the patient's consent.

It isn't unusual for people with eating disorders to resist or refuse treatment. As a result, symptoms of anorexia nervosa, bulimia nervosa, or other eating disorders may be present for months or even years before patients feel ready for change. These individuals are usually pressured by family members, friends, or coworkers to seek help, and often do so with reluctance and resentment.

According to Drs. Elliott M. Goldner and C. Laird Birmingham, and Victoria Smye . . . of the University of British Columbia, people struggling with eating disorders may have many reasons for refusing treatment. Some don't think they have an eating disorder at all and feel that their family or friends are exaggerating the problem or are mistaken about the symptoms.

Others may be well aware that they are struggling but are ashamed of their symptoms and afraid of being discovered. Many fear the potential effects of treatment, such as weight gain or interference with their drive to exercise, restrict food intake, purge, or lose weight.

Patients at Risk

In some cases, physicians must consider imposing treatment even when the patient actively resists. Individuals who may be at increased risk include: (1) young patients who have recently developed symptoms; (2) patients who are in immediate danger because of medical consequences of the illness or the risk of suicide; and (3) those with rapidly increasing symptoms.

When physicians decide to "order" treatment, they fully believe that treatment will be beneficial. Many patients in these situations are likely to benefit even if they don't recognize or support the plan.

> *People struggling with eating disorders may have many reasons for refusing treatment.*

When treatment is imposed against a person's wishes, the consequences may be great. Thus, physicians carefully weigh the potential benefits versus any risks before beginning. Sometimes, physical and chemical restraints are used, along with tube feeding and restriction of activity. In such settings, patients are often profoundly distressed and as a result avoid further treatment.

Legal Considerations

All jurisdictions have laws upholding the rights of individuals; thus, an individual's right to refuse treatment may be supported by the court. Minors and other individuals who are deemed incompetent (a legal term meaning that a person is mentally incapable of making his own decisions) may be temporarily denied the right to refuse treatment.

While they are competent in all other areas, individuals with eating disorders are often considered incompetent in certain specific areas of their lives, including decisions about their ability to gain weight or their current health and need for treatment. However, patients have a legal right to dispute this, and health-care providers must then turn to the legal system to support the need for imposed treatment. Other health-care providers will be asked to give a second opinion, and to estimate the risks involved if the patient were to have no treatment.

> *In some cases, physicians must consider imposing treatment even when the patient actively resists.*

Depending on the circumstances, individuals with eating disorders may be at risk of a number of life-threatening medical conditions. These conditions call for emergency assessment and response. Although medical professionals can identify an emergency situation in progress, it is hard to detect an impending medical crisis. Given the high rates of suicide in patients with eating disorders, a careful assessment of suicide risk should be undertaken.

Convincing the Patient to Accept Treatment

Because of the many consequences when a patient doesn't want to be treated, and the effects on families as well, health-care professionals often use a careful process in order to convince the patient to be treated before seeking legal means to accomplish this.

1. First, try to engage the patient in a voluntary partnership.

2. Explore the reasons that the patient is resisting treatment. It may be a fear of the unknown or he or she may be frightened by psychiatric or medical interventions in general. Other patients are severely depressed or have cognitive impairment. Most often, refusal to be treated is caused primarily by a cognitive disturbance or such things as a fear of gaining weight.

3. Before starting treatment, some facilities such as Dr. Goldner's use a preliminary intervention. During these sessions, his group provides information to the patients and family members, identifies goals of treatment, introduces staff members,

and talks about specific concerns a patient may have. They also thoroughly explain why a certain treatment is recommended, and what it is. This helps enhance motivation for change.

4. Involving the family in a realistic treatment plan usually improves the effects of therapy. Dr. Goldner's group uses a narrative approach to family interventions that is helpful in defusing family conflicts and lessening resistance to treatment. With narrative therapy, the family is encouraged and supported in developing a personal story, or "narrative" about recovery. This approach lessens power struggles and adapts treatment to the unique qualities and characteristics of each family.

5. Negotiations may be necessary. In order to promote the health and safety of the patient, professionals may need to make changes to the proposed treatment plan. Individuals with eating disorders are much more likely to respond to a professional who is approachable, flexible, and comfortable dealing with conflict.

6. All treatment plans should minimize the use of intrusive interventions, such as involuntary commitment to an inpatient unit, tube feeding or programs of behavior modification. Whenever possible, outpatient programs, day programs, and residential treatment should be used instead of inpatient treatment.

> **// When treatment is imposed against a person's wishes, the consequences may be great. //**

7. A realistic appraisal of the probable outcome of treatment versus no treatment will help guide the clinician to a rational plan. Imposing treatment should be considered only when the possible benefits outweigh the risks of not intervening.

8. Power struggles between the patient and the health-care team usually worsen symptoms and break down the therapeutic partnership. Patients who feel frightened or trapped may battle staff, have angry outbursts, or withdraw. It is important for health-care professionals to remain respectful and avoid threats or destructive criticism. Treatment should support self-esteem.

9. Due to potential risks, it is generally agreed that legal means of imposing treatment should be reserved for cases in which doing nothing would lead to a serious and immediate danger.

10. Patients who have struggled with eating disorders for a long time often need a different approach than those who have been ill for a shorter time. Chronic illness may indicate a particularly resistant eating disorder and it may be inappropriate to approach treatment of the chronic anorexic patient with a more aggressive plan for intervention.

11. Refusal or resistance to treatment can be viewed as an evolutionary process. Indeed, individuals who refuse treatment at first may later accept it. Usually the gradually increasing recognition of the negative impact of an eating disorder on a person's life is accompanied by a wish to recover. After refeeding has begun, patients may need less treatment due to improvements in emotional and cognitive processes.

Emergency Treatment Is Sometimes Needed

An individual with an eating disorder must be treated, even if she refuses, when any of the following signs and symptoms appear:
- Rapid weight loss, such as more than 15 lbs within 4 weeks
- Seizures
- Organic brain syndrome
- Slow heart rate (bradycardia, or fewer than 40 beats/minute)
- Other irregular heartbeats
- Frequent chest pain on exercise
- Volume depletion
- Painful muscle spasms (tetany)
- Quickly becoming tired while exercising
- Low urine output (less than 400 cc/day)
- Faintness
- Severe electrolyte imbalance

14

Family-Based Treatment Is Effective for Anorexics

James Lock

James Lock is a child and adolescent psychiatrist and assistant professor of child psychiatry at Stanford University School of Medicine. He is also medical director of the Comprehensive Pediatric Care Unit at Lucile Salter Packard Children's Hospital and codirector of the Adolescent Eating Disorder Program.

Studies of the available treatments for anorexia in teens indicate that inpatient treatment in a hospital or eating disorder clinic is likely to result in only short-term improvement. However, a relatively new family-based treatment developed at the Maudsley Hospital in London appears to hold the most promise for long-term recovery for teen sufferers of anorexia. Unlike most traditional therapies, which tend to exclude families from treatment, the Maudsley method emphasizes the importance of the family in refeeding and recovery.

A norexia nervosa is a serious psychiatric disorder that is estimated to have a prevalence of 0.48 percent among girls ages 15 to 19. Anorexia nervosa combines pathological thoughts and behaviors about food and weight with negative emotions concerning appearance, eating and food. These thoughts, feelings and behaviors lead to changes in body composition and functioning that are the direct result of starvation. As a result, among adolescents the illness severely affects physical, emotional and social development. In addition, there is a fair amount of evidence that suggests that anorexia nervosa often co-occurs with other psychiatric disorders including depression, anxiety disor-

James Lock, "Innovative Family-Based Treatment for Anorexia Nervosa," *Brown University Child and Adolescent Behavior Letter*, vol. 17, April 2001. Copyright © 2001 by Manisses Communications Group, Inc. Reproduced by permission.

ders, and obsessive-compulsive disorder.

It is not clear what causes anorexia nervosa. The mean age of onset is about 17 and many have suggested that the disorder represents the individual's difficulty negotiating the developmental demands of adolescence. Arthur Crisp's psychobiological perspective suggests that the symptoms of starvation and emaciation are attempts to cope with the demands of adolescence by regressing to an earlier developmental level. Hilda Bruch's psycho-dynamic formulation conceives of the patient as overwhelmed by feelings of ineffectiveness, emptiness and a concomitant inability to access his or her own thoughts, feelings and beliefs.

Anorexia and Adolescence

Recent research supports these ideas in the sense that eating problems initially emerge in response to pubertal change, especially fat accumulation. Other associated risks such as teasing by peers, discomfort in discussing problems with parents, maternal preoccupation with restricting dietary intake and acculturation to the Western values in immigrants also support the idea that adolescence itself is a key aspect of the illness.

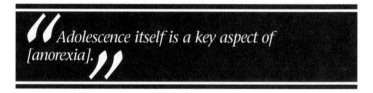

Adolescence itself is a key aspect of [anorexia].

Dieting and weight concerns are part of Western culture. Up to 60 to 70 percent of adolescent girls report such concerns. Therefore, it is important to distinguish between these predictable concerns and those that are more pathological. The DSM-IV [the Diagnostic and Statistical Manual of Mental Disorders] includes two different types of criteria for anorexia nervosa: medical and psychological. The medical criteria are the easiest to identify. Patients who are below 85 percent of ideal body weight (IBW) or who fail to make expected weight gains meet the weight criteria. The DSM also requires that three consecutive menstrual periods be missed in females who have reached menarche.

Psychological criteria include an intense "fear" of weight gain even though underweight and an overestimation of current body mass—usually called body-image distortion. Additionally, it is possible that anorexia nervosa may be complicated by binge-eating or purging behaviors.

Treatment Approaches Are Critical

Treatment of anorexia nervosa requires attention to the possibility of severe medical problems that commonly co-occur with the illness. Changes in growth hormone, hypothalamic hypogonadism, bone marrow hypoplasia, structural abnormalities of the brain, cardiac dysfunction, and gastrointestinal difficulties can occur. In addition, for adolescents there is the potential for significant growth retardation, pubertal delay or interruption, and peak bone mass reduction. Risks of death as a result of complications of anorexia nervosa are estimated at 6 to 15 percent, with half the deaths resulting from suicide. Thus, a therapist working with a patient with anorexia nervosa should ensure that they have adequate medical treatment and monitoring.

As might be expected, patients with anorexia nervosa sometimes require hospitalization. In fact, some data suggests that the total percent of time spent in hospitals by patients with anorexia nervosa is only exceeded by patients with schizophrenia. A variety of investigators have published reports on the effectiveness of inpatient hospitalization for acute treatment of anorexia nervosa. These studies demonstrate that inpatient treatment is likely to result in short-term improvement using a variety of clinical approaches, but because of increasing pressure to reduce the use of the modality due both to its high cost and its disruption of the adolescent's usual life, outpatient alternatives are increasingly stressed.

> *For adolescents, . . . family-based treatment is superior to individual therapy.*

There are only eight published outpatient treatment trials for anorexia nervosa. Fewer than 300 patients (or patients and their families) were treated in these controlled trials. Treatment approaches included nutritional advice, family therapy of different types, individual therapy, group therapy and cognitive and behavioral approaches.

The Maudsley Method

However insufficient this data, it appears that for adolescents with anorexia nervosa, a specific form of family therapy developed by Christopher Dare and Ivan Eisler at the Maudsley Hospital in London is the most promising. Studies of the Maudsley method demonstrate that for adolescents, this family-based treatment is superior to individual therapy and that five years after treatment its advantages continue to be evident.

The Maudsley method turns common presumptions about how to treat anorexia nervosa upside down. Historically, many therapists have seen families as pathological and interfering with the adolescent's ability to develop a sense of self. Thus, clinicians have blamed families, excluded them from treatment, and instead focused on the individual relationship of patient and therapist as the incubus for recovery. The focus of these types of treatments are on the conflicts or anxieties about adolescence that anorexia nervosa is helping them to avoid. The hope is that once the patient has an understanding of these problems, the patient will give up self-starvation.

> *The family is the best context in which to accomplish [re-feeding].*

In opposition to this view, the Maudsley method sees a patient in the acute starvation stages of anorexia nervosa as unable to use such insight until after a process of re-feeding has occurred. And perhaps even more importantly, the Maudsley method argues that the family is the best context in which to accomplish this.

The Family Is Not to Blame

The Maudsley method takes an agnostic view of the cause of anorexia nervosa, refusing to blame the family for the illness. Instead, the family is seen as the most important resource at the therapist's disposal. The therapist endeavors to empower them to take on the responsibility for nurturing their desperately ill child back to health. Accomplishing this task requires that the family be able to change its approach to the self-starvation that anorexia nervosa has imposed on their child.

In order to accomplish this arduous task, therapists schooled in the Maudsley method endeavor to place the family in a "therapeutic bind." On one side, the family is warned about the necessity for immediate action to prevent their child from succumbing to the illness—a terrifying thought that leads to increased anxiety, especially on the parent's part. On the other hand, in order to prevent this anxiety from becoming overwhelming, the therapist communicates acceptance, warmth and expertise to support the family.

> *The family is seen as the most important resource at the therapist's disposal.*

The Maudsley method owes its major components to a variety of clinicians and researchers. For example, family meals are employed in the treatment and used in a way similar to how [Salvador] Minuchin employed them in his treatment. The process of empowering the family to find their own solutions to their problems is based in the nonauthoritarian stance of Milan systems therapy as well as feminist theory. In order to assist the family in taking on the problems of anorexia nervosa without attacking their child, the Maudsley method emphasizes separating the patient from the illness, a technique based in part on narrative therapy strategies. Nonetheless, Dare's recipe is ultimately his own.

More research needs to be done examining the Maudsley method and it is also evident that clinicians outside of London need to become more familiar with the approach and be exposed to the techniques involved. Christopher Dare is one of the authors of a recently published treatment manual that provides a detailed description of his treatment approach. The manual provides a systematic account of the scientific literature supporting the use of family-based treatment for anorexia nervosa in adolescents and provides specific instructions in the methods used to engage families in this type of treatment. It also includes transcriptions of therapeutic sessions that illustrate how the treatment operates.

There are limitations to family-based treatment for anorexia nervosa ill adolescents. For example, data from the Maudsley studies show that this approach is less effective for older adolescents (over 18) or adults, adolescents who are chronically ill or those who binge and purge. In addition, highly critical families may not respond to the whole family treatment model and need alternative versions of family treatment to succeed.

There is a need to continue to evaluate this and other treatment approaches for anorexia nervosa, but family-based treatment based on the Maudsley model is the most promising treatment now available for helping adolescents with anorexia nervosa.

The Three Phases of the Maudsley Method

The Maudsley method for family-based therapy for adolescent anorexia nervosa has three clearly defined phases.

• In the first phase, the focus is on engaging the family and empowering them to re-feed their child. The therapist reinforces a strong parental alliance around re-feeding their offspring in order to help ensure success. At the same time, wishing not to abandon the adolescent to this process without support, the therapist attempts to align the patient with the sibling sub-system. The therapist directly expresses the view that parents did not cause the illness and compliments them as much as possible on their efforts.

• Phase two begins once the patient accepts the demands of the parents and steady weight gain is evident. The therapist focuses on encouraging the parents to help their child to take more control over eating herself [*sic*] as is appropriate for her age.

• Finally, the third phase begins when the patient is maintaining a stable weight (near 95 percent of his or her ideal) without significant parental supervision. Treatment focuses on the impact anorexia nervosa has had upon establishing a healthy adolescent identity. Then it is possible to review the central issues of adolescence, work toward increased personal autonomy for the adolescent, and more appropriate family boundaries. It should be noted that families have "learned by doing" in this therapy and are often in much better shape as a result of the changes they have made through their re-feeding efforts.

Organizations to Contact

The editors have compiled the following list of organizations concerned with the issues debated in this book. The descriptions are derived from materials provided by the organizations. All have publications or information available for interested readers. The list was compiled on the date of publication of the present volume; the information provided here may change. Be aware that many organizations take several weeks or longer to respond to inquiries, so allow as much time as possible.

Alliance for Eating Awareness
PO Box 13155, North Palm Beach, FL 33408-3155
(561) 841-0900 • fax: (561) 881-0380
e-mail: info@eatingdisorderinfo.org
Web site: www.eatingdisorderinfo.org

The Alliance for Eating Disorders Awareness seeks to establish easily accessible programs across the nation that provide children and young adults with the opportunity to learn about eating disorders and the positive effects of a healthy body image. It also disseminates educational information to parents and caregivers about the warning signs, dangers, and consequences of anorexia, bulimia, and other related disorders.

American Academy of Child and Adolescent Psychiatry (AACAP)
3615 Wisconsin Ave. NW, Washington, DC 20016
(202) 966-7300 • fax: (202) 966-2891
Web site: www.aacap.org

AACAP is a nonprofit organization dedicated to providing parents and families with information regarding developmental, behavioral, and mental disorders that affect children and adolescents. The organization provides national public information through the distribution of the newsletter *Facts for Families* and the monthly *Journal of the American Academy of Child and Adolescent Psychiatry*.

American Psychiatric Association (APA)
1000 Wilson Blvd., Suite 1825, Arlington, VA 22209-3901
(703) 907-7300
e-mail: apa@psych.org • Web site: www.psych.org

APA is an organization of psychiatrists dedicated to studying the nature, treatment, and prevention of mental disorders. It helps create mental health policies, distributes information about psychiatry, and promotes psychiatric research and education. APA publishes the monthly *American Journal of Psychiatry*.

American Psychological Association
750 First St. NE, Washington, DC 20002-4242
(202) 336-5500 • fax: (202) 336-5708
e-mail: public.affairs@apa.org • Web site: www.apa.org

This society of psychologists aims to advance psychology as a science, as a profession, and as a means of promoting human welfare. It produces numerous publications, including the monthly journal *American Psychologist*, the monthly newspaper *APA Monitor*, and the quarterly *Journal of Abnormal Psychology*.

Anna Westin Foundation
112329 Chatfield Ct., Chaska, MN 55318
(952) 361-3051 • fax: (952) 448-4036
e-mail: kitty@annawestinfoundation.org
Web site: www.annawestinfoundation.org

The Anna Westin Foundation is dedicated to the prevention and treatment of eating disorders. The foundation is committed to preventing the loss of life to anorexia nervosa and bulimia, and to raising public awareness of these dangerous illnesses. In addition, the foundation champions the cause of complete health insurance coverage for eating disorder treatment. Information about anorexia and bulimia are available on the Web site.

Anorexia Nervosa and Related Eating Disorders, Inc. (ANRED)
PO Box 5102, Eugene, OR 97405
(503) 344-1144
e-mail: jarinor@rio.com • Web site: www.anred.com

ANRED is a nonprofit organization that provides information about anorexia nervosa, bulimia nervosa, binge eating disorder, compulsive exercising, and other lesser-known food and weight disorders, including details about recovery and prevention. ANRED offers workshops, individual and professional training, as well as local community education. It also produces a monthly newsletter.

Center for the Study of Anorexia and Bulimia (CSAB)
1841 Broadway, 4th Fl., New York, New York 10023
(212) 333-3444 • fax: (212) 333-5444
e-mail: info@csabnyc.org • Web site: www.csabnyc.org

CSAB is a division of the Institute for Contemporary Psychotherapy. It is the oldest nonprofit eating disorder clinic in New York City and is devoted to treating individuals with eating disorders and training the professionals who work with them. CSAB also provides help and counseling for families of eating disordered individuals. Information, reading lists, and links to other resources are available on the CSAB Web site.

Eating Disorder Education Organization (EDEO)
6R20 Edmonton General Hospital
11111 Jesper Ave., Edmonton, AB T5K 0L4 Canada
(780) 944-2864
e-mail: info@edeo.org • Web site: www.edeo.org

The Eating Disorder Education Organization of Edmonton is a non-profit human rights organization celebrating human diversity. EDEO's primary objective is to increase the awareness of eating disorders and their prevalence throughout society. Through education and outreach, the organization encourages people to develop a positive self image based on ability and personality rather than just physical appearance and to understand that weight is not a measure of self-worth. EDEO publishes a monthly online bulletin and provides speakers to schools and organizations.

Eating Disorders Coalition for Research, Policy, and Action (EDC)
611 Pennsylvania Ave. SE, #423, Washington, DC 20003-4303
(202) 543-9570 • fax: (202) 543-9570
e-mail: EDCoalition@aol.com
Web site: www.eatingdisorderscoalition.org

The EDC mission is to advance federal recognition of eating disorders as a public health priority. Their priorities are to increase resources for research, education, prevention, and improved training; promote federal support for improved access to care; and promote initiatives that support the healthy development of children. EDC publishes reports and policy recommendation as well as a monthly online newsletter.

Harvard Eating Disorders Center (HEDC)
WACC 725, 15 Parkman St., Boston, MA 02114
(617) 726-8470
Web site: www.hedc.org

HEDC is a national nonprofit organization dedicated to research and education. It works to expand knowledge about eating disorders and their detection, treatment, and prevention, and promotes the health of everyone at risk of developing a eating disorder. A primary goal for the organization is lobbying for health policy initiatives on behalf of individuals with eating disorders.

National Association of Anorexia Nervosa and Associated Disorders (ANAD)
Box 7, Highland Park, IL 60035
(847) 831-3438 • fax: (847) 433-4632
e-mail: info@anad.org • Web site: www.anad.org

ANAD offers hotline counseling, operates an international network of support groups for people with eating disorders and their families, and provides referrals to health care professionals who treat eating disorders. It produces a quarterly newsletter and information packets and organizes national conferences and local programs. All ANAD services are provided free of charge.

National Eating Disorder Information Centre (NEDIC)
ES 7-421, 200 Elizabeth St., Toronto, ON M5G 2C4 Canada
(416) 340-4156 • fax: (416) 340-4736
e-mail: nedic@uhn.on.ca • Web site: www.nedic.on.ca

NEDIC provides information and resources on eating disorders and weight preoccupation, and it focuses on the sociocultural factors that influence female-health-related behaviors. NEDIC promotes healthy lifestyles and encourages individuals to make informed choices based on accurate information. It publishes a newsletter and a guide for families and friends of eating-disorder sufferers and sponsors Eating Disorders Awareness Week in Canada.

National Eating Disorders Association (NEDA)
603 Stewart St., Suite 803, Seattle, WA 98101
(206) 382-3587 • fax: (206) 829-8501
e-mail: info@nationaleatingdisoders.org
Web site: www.nationaleatingdisorders.org

The National Eating Disorders Association is the largest not-for-profit organization in the United States working to prevent eating disorders and provide treatment referrals to those suffering from anorexia, bulimia, and binge-eating disorders, and those concerned with body image and weight issues. NEDA also provides educational outreach programs and training for schools and universities and sponsors the Puppet Project for Schools and the annual National Eating Disorders Awareness Week. NEDA publishes a prevention curriculum for grades four through six as well as public prevention and awareness information packets, videos, guides, and other materials.

Bibliography

Books

Marlene Boskind-White and William C. White Jr.	*Bulimia/Anorexia: The Binge/Purge Cycle and Self-Starvation.* New York: W.W. Norton, 2000.
Hilde Bruch	*The Golden Cage: The Enigma of Anorexia Nervosa.* Cambridge, MA: Harvard University Press, 2001.
Joan Jacobs Brumberg	*Fasting Girls: The History of Anorexia Nervosa.* New York: Vintage Books, 2000.
Julie M. Clarke and Ann Kirby-Payne	*Understanding Weight and Depression.* New York: Rosen, 2000.
Julia K. De Pree	*Body Story.* Athens, OH: Swallow Press/Ohio University Press, 2004.
Kathlyn Gay	*Eating Disorders: Anorexia, Bulimia, and Binge Eating.* Berkeley Heights, NJ: Enslow, 2003.
Tracey Gold	*Room to Grow: An Appetite for Life.* Beverly Hills, CA: New Millennium Press, 2003.
Richard A. Gordon	*Eating Disorders: Anatomy of a Social Epidemic.* Malden, MA: Blackwell, 2000.
Lori Gottlieb	*Stick Figure: A Diary of My Former Self.* New York: Berkley Books, 2001.
Bonnie B. Graves	*Anorexia.* Mankato, MN: LifeMatters, 2000.
Tania Heller	*Eating Disorders: A Handbook for Teens, Families, and Teachers.* Jefferson, NC: McFarland, 2003.
Jennifer Hendricks	*Slim to None: A Journey Through the Wasteland of Anorexia Treatment.* Chicago: Contemporary Books, 2003.
Marlys C. Johnson	*Understanding Exercise Addiction.* New York: Rosen, 2000.
Cynthia R. Kalodner	*Too Fat or Too Thin? A Reference Guide to Eating Disorders.* Westport, CT: Greenwood Press, 2003.
Jim Kirkpatrick and Paul Caldwell	*Eating Disorders: Anorexia Nervosa, Bulimia, Binge Eating, and Others.* Buffalo, NY: Firefly Books, 2001.
Caroline Knapp	*Appetites: Why Women Want.* New York: Counterpoint, 2003.
Nancy J. Kolodny	*The Beginner's Guide to Eating Disorders Recovery.* Carlsbad, CA: Gurze Books, 2004.

Steven Levenkron	*Anatomy of Anorexia.* New York: W.W. Norton, 2000.
Alexander R. Lucas	*Demystifying Anorexia Nervosa: An Optimistic Guide to Understanding and Healing.* New York: Oxford University Press, 2004.
Dawn D. Matthews, ed.	*Eating Disorders Sourcebook: Basic Consumer Information About Eating Disorders Including Information About Anorexia Nervosa.* Detroit: Omnigraphics, 2001.
Morgan Menzie	*Diary of an Anorexic Girl.* Nashville: W, 2003.
Deborah Marcontell Michel	*When Dieting Becomes Dangerous: A Guide to Understanding and Treating Anorexia and Bulimia.* New Haven, CT: Yale University Press, 2003.
Heather Moehn	*Understanding Eating Disorder Support Groups.* New York: Rosen, 2000.
Christie Pettit	*Starving: A Personal Journey Through Anorexia.* Grand Rapids, MI: F.H. Revell, 2003.
Linda M. Rio and Tara M. Rio	*The Anorexia Diaries: A Mother and Daughter's Triumph over Teenage Eating Disorders.* Emmaus, PA: Rodale, 2003.
Tammie Ronen	*In and Out of Anorexia: The Story of the Client, the Therapist, and the Process of Recovery.* London and Philadelphia: Jessica Kingsley, 2001.
Ira M. Sacker	*Dying to Be Thin: Understanding and Defeating Anorexia Nervosa and Bulimia.* New York: Warner Books, 2001.
Debbie Stanley	*Understanding Sports and Eating Disorders.* New York: Rosen, 2000.

Periodicals

Karen Dias	"The Ana Sanctuary: Women's Pro-Anorexia Narratives in Cyberspace," *Journal of International Women's Studies,* April 2003.
Deirdre Dolan	"Learning to Love Anorexia? Pro-Ana Web Sites Flourish," *New York Observer,* July 29, 2004.
Marian Fitzgibbon and Melinda Stolley	"Minority Women: The Untold Story," *NOVA Online,* December 2000. www.pbs.org/wgbh/nova/thin/minorities.html.
Tamsin Ford and Anthony Kessel	"Feeling the Way: Childhood Mental Illness and Consent to Admission and Treatment," *British Journal of Psychiatry,* 2001.
Doug Grow	"Couple Helped Hatch Spar with Blue Cross," *Minneapolis Star Tribune,* June 20, 2001.
Harvard Mental Health Letter	"Anorexia Nervosa, Part II," March 2003.

Bruce Jancin — "Anxiety Disorders, Depression Found in Former Anorexics," *Clinical Psychiatry News*, August 2003.

Journal of the American Dietetic Association — "Position of the American Dietetic Association: Nutrition Intervention in the Treatment of Anorexia Nervosa, Bulimia Nervosa, and Eating Disorders Not Otherwise Specified (EDNOS)," July 2001.

Allan S. Kaplan — "Compulsory Refeeding in Anorexia: Beneficial or Harmful?" *Journal of Addiction and Mental Health*, May/June 2002.

E. Grace Lager and Brian R. McGee — "Hiding the Anorectic: A Rhetorical Analysis of Popular Discourse Concerning Anorexia," *Women's Studies in Communication*, Fall 2003.

Chris MacDonald — "Treatment Resistance in Anorexia Nervosa and the Pervasiveness of Ethics in Clinical Decision Making," *Canadian Journal of Psychiatry*, April 2002.

Jim McCaffree — "Eating Disorders: All in the Family," *Journal of the American Dietetic Association*, June 2001.

Claudia Miller — "Boys Who Binge: Increasing Number in North Bay Vulnerable to Eating Disorders," *San Francisco Chronicle*, December 15, 2000.

Peggy O'Farrell — "Anorexia Increasing, Treatment Shrinking: Families Struggle Against Eating Disorder," *Cincinnati Enquirer*, September 5, 2002.

Terry O'Neill — "Death Wish I: Dying to be Skeletal, *Report Newsmagazine*, January 21, 2002.

Susan Schindehette — "Recipe for Life: A Breakthrough Therapy Brings Hope to Young Girls—and the Families—Who Suffer from Anorexia," *People Weekly*, December 15, 2003.

Carrie Myers Smith — "Eating Disorders and Pregnancy," *IDEA Health and Fitness Source*, May 2000.

Theodore E. Weltzin — "Male Eating Disorders," *EAP Association Exchange*, September/October 2001.

Theodore E. Weltzin — "Unique Inpatient Program Treating Boys with Eating Disorders," *Brown University Child and Adolescent Behavior Letter*, March 2002.

Index

108